How to Tell When You're Tired

A Brief Examination of Work

Reg Theriault

W · W · Norton & Company

New York   London

How to Tell When You're Tired

A Brief Examination of Work

The text of this book is composed in 11/13.5 Bembo
with the display set in Lucian Bold
Composition by The Maple-Vail Book Composition Services
Manufacturing by The Maple-Vail Manufacturing Group
Book design by Margaret M. Wagner

Excerpt from "Questions From A Worker Who Reads" in Selected
Poems, copyright 1947 by Bertolt Brecht and H. R. Hays and reviewed
1975 by Stefan S. Brecht and H. R. Hays, reprinted by permission of
Harcourt Brace and Company.

Chapter 12, "Three Decades on the Frisco Waterfront," was originally issued
as a pamphlet in the labor series published by Singlejack Press, San Pedro, CA.

Library of Congress Cataloging-in-Publication Data
Theriault, Reg, 1924–
How to tell when you're tired : a brief examination of work / by
Reg Theriault.
p. cm.
1. Work.   2. Work—Psychological
aspects.   3. Labor.   4. Labor—
Psychological aspects.   I. Title.
HD4901.T477   1995
306.3'6—dc20   95–2152

ISBN 978-0-393-31557-8

W. W. Norton & Company, Inc., 500 Fifth Avenue, New York, N.Y. 10110
W. W. Norton & Company Ltd., 10 Coptic Street, London WC1A 1PU

Contents

Who built Thebes of the seven gates?
In the books the kings are named,
But who hauled the rock?
And Babylon, many times demolished,
Who raised it again? In what houses
Of gold-glittering Lima did the builders live?
Where, when the Great Wall of China was finally
    done,
Did the masons go?

—BERTOLT BRECHT
    "Questions from a Worker
    Who Reads"

Preface

There have been many volumes published on work, but very little has been written by those who do it. What does it mean to work all your life at hard, physical labor? Even now, with holidays, weekends, and vacations, time off is little more than a respite; we all know that work is there waiting for us Monday morning. Work is the cardinal fact of working men's and working women's existence.

Work, for most of mankind, is something to avoid if possible. Not merely avoid but, if you are powerful enough or have money enough, arrange for someone else to do for you. Work always has to be done. Among those working people at the bottom of the labor heap, trapped in drudgery and perhaps powerless to escape, getting "promoted" to an easier job is never far from their minds. I, who have had choices, would be less than honest if I did not admit that these same thoughts have occurred to me any number of times on the jobs I've held down over the years. But even with all the undeniable onerousness and, yes, sometimes even pure pain that can accompany hard labor, work and working with other workers, have returned to me rewards and fulfillments that have kept me committed to it as the way I make my living. This has been true for many other workers I know. This book is an attempt to explain why.

The industrial revolution created something new in the worlds, the industrial blue-collar worker. The former serf, peasant, or town laborer, whose former obedience and loyalty to his lord or craft master had been unquestioned, now newly tending his machine in the production process, found himself in an adversarial position in relation to those who owned the factory in which he worked. Ideologies, mainly socialist or communist, came into being to champion and empower this new industrial worker and govern in his name. Whatever their success or lack of it, what is significant is that after almost two-hundred years, industrial work largely resembles itself wherever you choose to observe it, under whatever ideology, throughout the world. This book is also about that.

REG THERIAULT
March 1995

How to
Tell
When
You're
Tired

A Brief
Examination
of Work

CHAPTER ONE

Genesis

Work has always been with us. In the Old Testament, Adam, meaning mankind, was condemned to live all the days of his life by the sweat of his brow. No definitive instructions came down with this brief, undeniably angry command, and so God, if indeed it was He who issued the order, left a multitude of puzzling questions that remain unanswered to this day. If He meant *all* mankind, then how come some people are working their asses off while others can't even find a job, and still others get to idle their life away living off the interest from tax-free municipal bonds? And *condemned?* As if work were a death penalty waiting to be carried out at the end of a life of joyless, backbreaking toil. I have worked all my life doing hard physical labor, and I and all the people with whom I have worked have, at least at times, found our jobs interesting and rewarding, and occasionally even fun. There have been other times, of course, when I labored long and hard at cruel, repetitious drudgery and thought the day would never end. This book is about what it is like to do both.

Work originally meant moving weight. When that first hunter continued pursuing the deer long after the rest of the tribe had given up the chase, he found himself with a unique problem when he finally brought the animal down: he had to transport the carcass back to the cave. Even if he was a strong man and it was a small deer and he could easily throw the animal up across his shoulders when he started out, he soon discovered that carrying it was tough going. No wonder. Being the very first man to move weight other than his own, he was the first person in the world to *work*. For better or worse, his acceptance of toil introduced a condition into life that most of the people on earth have accepted ever since.

In a primitive sense, work is picking something up and putting it down somewhere else because you have to. If the object is heavy, moving it is called *hard* work. There aren't many people around packing deer for a living anymore, but there are still a lot of us picking up heavy cases, or hundred-pound sacks of wheat, barley, coffee, rice, or whatever, and stacking them up on pallet boards or on the bed of a truck or in the hold of a ship.

Probably a lot more people are doing what might be called *light* work. But if light work means picking up light things, that can be a misnomer, because often it is harder to pick up a large number of light objects than a few heavy ones, especially if you have to bend down to get them.

Some work is called skilled and some of it unskilled, although you do not often hear a worker use those terms. If "unskilled" is applied to work which requires little or no training or preparation, it too fails its definition, as anyone who has just got through moving his first refrigerator knows.

In spite of automation, most of the people across the

face of this earth are doing work, much of it hard work, most of the days of their lives. Whether they like it or not is another question. Like it or not, work is something they have to do, and it is still as true today as it ever was that by the time most kids are big enough or old enough or educated enough to get their first job, they are already conditioned, by the example of their fathers if they are boys, to pass beyond liking or disliking work to accepting it as inevitable.

My first job was in a packing shed in the lower San Joaquin Valley of California. My people were fruit tramps. That is, we were itinerant, migratory agricultural workers, following the crops summer through spring from town to town and sometimes even from state to state. I had arrived at the age, fifteen, when it was time for me to go to work, so I braced the foreman for a job on the cantaloupe shed where my father was a packer. It was well into the harvest, the packing shed was working night and day, and, luckily for me, they needed *men*. The boss, after giving me a doubtful look (I was an undersized, skinny kid), led me back past the packers and sorters and loaders to the rear of the shed. Down on the ground below us another skinny kid, not much different from me, was busy at a bench making crates.

"Can you nail?" the boss asked me above the noise of the cull chute, a conveyor belt running directly over our heads carrying out overripe and rotten melons to a waiting dump truck. "Do you know how to use a handax?"

Standing there looking down at the box maker, whose back was to us, I didn't know what kind of a lie to tell. A nailing ax, like any other hatchet, has a handle and a blade, but the other end of the head, the working end, has a square, knurled surface which is used for driving nails; the

blade is used only for counterbalance. I had never put
together a crate before in my life, but I knew immediately
that if I got the job and joined the box maker below us I
would start out at no less than approximately even. The
other kid's performance even let me grab at an arrogant
hope that, next to him, I might even look *good*. When he
hit the nail, which wasn't all that often, he frequently
drove it in crooked and bent over the head. The slats on
the sides of his completed crates, instead of running paral-
lel to each other, angled off every which way. Finally, he
wasn't very fast. Fairness compelled me to grant him one
small excuse, however. The cull chute, rushing the tum-
bling cantaloupes along above our heads, would occasionally toss out a stray melon. Upon hitting the ground the
melon would shatter, broadcasting seeds and juice about
in a wide arc. This was attracting a lot of flies. A good
many of the flies were swarming around the box maker's
head, trying to light on his ears, which stuck out. In
between driving nails he would violently shake his head,
throwing off sweat and flies, but the flies, like the sweat,
would immediately return. Now and then he would
hunch his shoulders and shudder, which was more of a
comment than a measure of relief.

"I need somebody to help him out," the foreman said
loudly in my ear. "I'll pay you five cents a crate for every
crate you make." Suddenly, as we watched, the kid
hunched his shoulders, savagely shook his head, and, in an
unthinking fit of torment, swung the ax up in the wrong
direction. The blade opened up about a two-inch gash on
his cheek just forward of his right ear. After a moment of
rigid stillness, the boy dropped the ax, staggered around
in a circle, and sat down. My first job.

I took over from someone who was, no doubt about it,

literally knocking himself out. In the following weeks I did not do exactly that, but I must have done any number of things equally dumb. I also inherited the flies. But all that was of no importance. It was a long time ago and it certainly was not much of a job, but I remember that as that foreman led me back past all the other busy workers I wanted to go to work on that packing shed more than anything else on earth. In the following weeks the other workers let me ride with them, eat with them, and listen to their stories. I couldn't drink with them, because I was too young to get into a bar, but they didn't hold that against me.

Most crates were nailed together by machine, even in those days, and I was making special crates for smaller melons. After a while that job was discontinued and I was put to work up on the shed, trucking full crates of cantaloupes into the railroad cars. It was a much harder job, but I could not have been happier. Now I was working with other people. What better way could you think of to spend the day? As soon as it was seen that I could handle the new job, I was accepted completely, and even my cussing quickly lost its apologetic tone. The other workers, especially the loaders, still expected me to listen. But what of that? After all, at that age what stories could I possibly have to tell?

Nailing those crates together was regarded as lowly work. I suppose it would be natural to dismiss it as a mere job, the first of the very many I have held down over the years. But that job that summer has remained the most important thing that ever happened to me in my life because of what I felt about it. I had become a man.

Chapter Two

Such Were the Joys

For a period of about eighty years, starting shortly after the beginning of our century, a group of nomads wandered over the western states of America harvesting crops. They called themselves fruit tramps, and I was born into their number.

Their origin was in the Pacific Northwest, and the railroad created them. Actually, the railroad doubly created them: first, by spanning the continent the rails offered a nationwide market for fresh fruits and produce, fostering megafarms and huge orchards rather than a myriad of small, family-run truck farms servicing small local markets; and second, by providing a means of transportation they enabled harvest hands in mega-numbers to get to where they were needed, to where the work was. Fruit tramps were America's first hobos.

By 1915 the Washington State apple crop was the largest in America. The refrigerator car, essentially nothing more than an insulated boxcar with bunkers for ice at both ends, made apples and other fruit and produce available to every corner of America. For three months every fall in Washington State, there was work for everyone who wanted it. Hard work.

After the orchard is planted and starts bearing fruit, the apple industry goes through three stages annually. In the spring after the blossoms have fallen, someone on a ladder goes down each limb of every tree in the orchard knocking a selected one-third of the emerging little knobby green fruit to the ground. This thinning is done so that the remaining apples will grow to a larger, more attractive, more valuable size. In early fall, crews drag the same ladders back into the orchard and pick the ripening fruit, depositing the apples in long canvas sacks hanging down from their chests almost to their knees. When a sack is full—a sack holds sixty or seventy pounds of apples—the picker climbs down the ladder and dumps the apples into a lug box, in which they are transported to the packing shed. Washing, sorting, and packing the apples into boxes for transportation for market completes the third stage.

Apples now are merely washed, coated with a clear plastic sealer to preserve them, and sent to market loosely dumped in a cardboard box. Until recently, however, apples, as well as oranges, tomatoes, peaches, pears, and some melons, were individually wrapped in tissue paper and precisely packed in wooden crates or boxes. The tissue paper kept the one apple that went bad from contaminating the whole box.

When the harvest began, all the local people the packing houses could muster were hired first. Transients, and not just those guys off the freight trains, were put to work only as they were needed—that is, when the fruit ripened in such quantities that it began to "snow" apples. The selection process reinforced and increased the already existing animosity between the "home guards" and the fruit tramps, making it tough to present a solid front when you went up against the boss demanding more money.

About the same time apples became a growth industry in Washington, the acreage of citrus groves began doubling annually in Southern California, as did the acreage devoted to peaches, pears, and tomatoes in other parts of the state. When the apple harvest was through in November, the navel oranges were starting to show color in the south. Freight trains ran in that direction, too, and, hell, what better way to spend the winter than in sunny Southern California? In the case of my family—my mother, father, sister, brother, and me—our transportation to the Golden State was a Model T Ford with missing side curtains and a fabric top. All our possessions were packed onto the running boards—in apple boxes, what else? Two spare tires hung down from the back of the automobile.

The varied climate of California permits the growth of one agricultural commodity or another throughout the year—oranges in winter and spring, peaches in midsummer, pears somewhat later, lettuce and tomatoes just about the year round. And there were always those apples every fall back in Washington. This quickly created a group of workers who followed the crops. It was always piecework, and the speed and ability workers acquired packing one commodity was easily applied to the next.

The single, rough itinerant male of the early days gave way to families as those men found wives, usually from among the ranks of the home guards, women to whom, apparently, the fruit tramps didn't seem so bad after all. Group identification quickly developed, and an internal cohesion fostered by the remnants of the hobo / Wobbly ideology enabled the workers to enforce demands and raise their pay to a living wage. The shippers and growers on one side and the fruit tramps on the other, however, remained adversarial to the end. The employers would have much preferred not to use fruit tramps, but when the snow hit, who else was willing to work twelve or fourteen hours, day in and day out, to save the crop?

To a kid growing up, the fruit tramp life meant changing schools three to five times a year, some years more. Among my earliest memories are leaving, in early morning, the Imperial Valley, or the lower San Joaquin, and moving north, winding up one job and heading for another. I was the youngest of three, and my position in the car, now a closed sedan, was the ledge in front of the back window, where I would lie crosswise, staring out at the receding highway.

People tend to express dismay when they discover the circumstances of my grammar and high school education, but I have to acknowledge that I never felt disadvantaged or deprived, either while I was growing up or later. I was always apprehensive, of course, when faced with a new school and strange people—once in a small town in the central San Joaquin Valley the school authorities attempted to segregate the three of us from their own, mainstream children—but frequently I would be returning to renewed friendships in schools I had attended the year before. And there were always other fruit tramp kids. Unquestionably our education was fragmented. For instance, I never learned to do long division; I left one school just as the class was beginning that subject, and arrived at another just as its class had finished. Traveling stretched out across the window ledge was mostly boring, but every now and then truck drivers would wave back at me when we passed them on the highway.

I started working rather young, mostly in summer and, until I achieved some growth, always in the fields or orchards. No self-respecting fruit tramp of the old blood would pick anything for a living once he had made it up to a job on the shed. I was no exception. When I finally made it I felt as if I had successfully completed a rite of passage. I had arrived.

Mostly because of our mother's relentless insistence, the three of us graduated from high school. Later, thanks to the GI Bill, I went on to college, bouncing around there, too, from one institution to another until I finally ended up at Berkeley. With the doggedness of someone who had been denied schooling herself, my mother prodded me toward an education, even picking out a course of study for me. I was to become an engineer. What kind, she really had no idea. I think it must have been that she thought being an engineer was as remote as one could get from being a fruit tramp, which she regarded as less than the epitome of success.

I was a pathetic failure in the field of her choice. With or without long division I had no aptitude for science, and when I managed, all in one semester, to flunk physics, chemistry, and mathematics, I knew my course of studies was hopeless. What I really liked to do, I realized, was read. So to hell with calculus; when I enrolled at Cal it was as an English major.

I supplemented the GI Bill and actually supported myself in comparative comfort all winter in Berkeley by heading back to the packing sheds and fruit tramping all summer. Starting in Yuma, Arizona, in early June, and then working my way north, I packed cantaloupes until the fall semester started in mid-September. After three summers of this routine I found myself enrolling the following fall with a certain reluctance. By mid-semester, I knew I was through. I had had it with the university, and any university. I was urged to remain in school by everyone with whom I had studied except one man, the brightest star in Berkeley's then star-studded English Department. Whether he saw me as a poor candidate for an eventual teaching post or had some vicarious investment in what he perceived to be my wild, adventuresome life, a life that he had never had, he did not discourage me from leaving Cal. He bought me lunch, wished me luck, and said goodbye. He may have known something. To this day I have never regretted it.

I went back to fruit tramping, following the same life my mother and father had led. Eventually, I married and had sons. As time went on, however, it became evident that the days of our lives as fruit tramps were numbered. With hardly a warning, there was no work in the winter. Instead of being hauled into town to the sheds, lettuce began to be packed in the fields. And instead of using fruit tramps, the growers imported Mexican braceros to do the work. For almost half of the year I had to find work elsewhere, usually in light industry in the San Francisco Bay Area, but every spring I was off again. When we worked, we fruit tramps continued to make good money, very good at times, but other changes were taking place. Living out of a suitcase, especially with kids, was becoming increasingly expensive. Perhaps working all day and half the night in Yuma, where the temperature reached 114 degrees, was beginning to take its toll, too. Consequently, when I got a chance to go to work on the San Francisco waterfront as a longshoreman, I promptly gave it a try.

Longshoring gave me and the family a good income and stability. It also provided something that was lacking in the factories where I had worked, something that fruit tramping had and that I missed. On my second day on the piers I was dispatched to a job working with an old-timer on a forklift who was relaying loads of lumber to the ship. My job consisted mostly of picking up and putting down blocks of wood, four-by-fours, under the loads so he could slip the blades of the forklift in and out. About two hours into the morning, after the old-timer and I came back to the job from a coffee break, he pointed to the lift.

"Here, kid," he said. (Kid? I was approaching my mid-thirties.) "You drive this thing and I'll put down blocks for a while." I had driven a forklift before, but not moving cargo like this. The lumber was eighteen feet long and extended out on both sides of the lift like the wings on a Boeing 747. I took it slow, and teetered a lot, but I kept up with the hook carrying the lumber into the hold of the ship and I did not spill a single load.

Just before noon the walking boss suddenly showed up. He confronted the old-timer, who had been enjoying himself as much as I had, shooting the breeze with the hook-on men on the dock beside the ship and eating walnuts he had found in the cargo somewhere on the pier.

"What the hell you doin' here, Cecil?" the walking boss demanded. "You're supposed to be the forklift driver on this job. Not this guy."

"Yeah?" the old-timer answered, deliberately taking his time. "Well, if you don't like the way me and the kid here work, we'll go back to the hiring hall and get us a dispatch to some other dock."

I had found another home.

After I began longshoring, for the next sixteen years I would slip away from the waterfront each summer and return to fruit tramping. Eventually I took my three sons with me and they got jobs on the packing sheds, too (also lying about their ages, of course). But fruit tramping as we had known it was obviously doomed. A way of life that began with the century was not going to last it out. Imported labor and new, genetically engineered fruit and vegetables were doing it in. Aliens, in America only to work provisionally (or perhaps here illegally), are docile employees and sell their labor cheap. They have become the corporate farmers' choice. Tomatoes, peaches, cantaloupes, you name it, are today selectively bred to be tough. Instead of packing them carefully you can now simply dump them into a container and ship them east. They do not bruise and they arrive at the market looking beautiful, though they are somewhat rubbery and lacking in taste. A few fruit tramps hang on. But of my extended family of over a dozen people, only one nephew continues to follow the crops.

The waterfront and I fit perfectly together. What I had started tentatively as perhaps merely another job became my life's work for over three decades. As a longshoreman I would be dispatched to a different pier every day or two. A long job was five days to load out a ship—and I was freer of the tedium of routine than even a fruit tramp could hope for. Both occupations had their share of hard work; cotton or coffee, depending on what hatch you were working on the ship, could be pure hell. But the next day I might catch a job placing wood blocks under loads of lumber for a forklift driver, the easiest job on the waterfront. What made the switch to longshoring so natural for me, however, was the remarkable similarity of the two work forces. I immediately recognized that crusty old-timer on the forklift truck. Every packing shed I ever worked on had a solid core of men and women like him, independent, ready to quit or pull a wildcat strike over wages or working conditions *at any time*. I quickly discovered that the waterfront was amply supplied with them, too.

CHAPTER THREE

Now We're Just Going to Make a Few Changes Here and There

For a factory worker in America, breakfast each morning will very likely come from a menu as varied as those foods available from the local supermarket's shelves. However, it is a universal truth, well acknowledged, that man, woman, does not live by bread alone. The best-paid artisan, however plump, in a clean, warm, well-lighted factory, enjoying a contractually defined workday, can hold within himself such feelings of anger that he will thrust a sabot into the well-oiled gears of his workplace, and thus bring the machinery to a halt. What may prompt him to this action, or to hold it in check, is at best only slightly understood by those who own the means of production.

The continued bounty from that supermarket is, of course, always a constant factor in labor peace, but the compelling drive for increased profits by management can nudge a worker toward the point where he lifts a leg and reaches for a shoe. And it can happen with the appearance of something as innocuous as a clipboard.

Back in the middle 1920s, about the time that American industry began seriously to entertain time-and-motion studies, a group of scientists were hired to undertake a project in a plant in Illinois that manufactured communications equipment. The purpose of the project was to determine the relationship between working conditions and productivity. That is, to see what could be done for, or against, the people who worked there so that they would assemble more switchboards, telephone receivers, and dialing units.

My own experience with management is that managers are not necessarily cruel or hostile; they simply are interested in production. More production, of course. If managers have a choice between dangling a carrot in front of you and using a whip to get you to work harder, they much prefer the carrot, but they will use either. In most places I have worked they use both.

The research in this factory was done by a well-financed team of sociologists and psychologists from two of our foremost universities, and extreme care was taken to conduct an honest, clinical, and objective study. Elaborate guidelines were laid down to eliminate human bias and error, and a number of graduate students were employed to take notes and do time-and-motion studies.

The project was begun in two sections of the factory at the same time, and the initial experiment was to alter the lighting and relief breaks, a euphemism for going to the toilet. A fifteen-minute relief break twice a day in one department was compared to five minutes off each hour in the other. The lighting was worked over so that it could be brightened or dimmed at will, and loudspeakers were installed to broadcast music into the workplaces. Additional changes were made in the environment as time went on, but the total hours worked were kept the same—you can bet your sweet life management saw to that.

As the data came in it was analyzed and correlated, and as months went by the results were not so much revealing as puzzling. If a fifteen-minute relief break, bright lights, and rousing Sousa marches saw a production week of, say, 12,012 dialing units in Department A, and dim bulbs, an hour lunch, and Viennese waltzes contributed to 12,001 in Department B, what was to be made of the following week when a reversal of the conditions saw an increase in Department B to 12,054 while Department A remained almost static at 12,009? Production in one department dropped, finally, when the lighting was reduced to the point where the workers couldn't see their workbenches clearly. The only solid trend noted going into the second year of study was that employee absenteeism increased in late spring and summer and also around the time of the World Series. What appeared at the start to be a straightforward task of collecting data and drawing conclusions from a set of facts had proved over a period of time to have complications and subtleties that were, on the face of it, simply inexplicable. Accordingly, more funds were acquired, more staff hired, and more studies begun, probably into the age, sex, and ethnic background of the employees in Department B.

The study was well into its second year when late one afternoon a young graduate student, wandering around among the workbenches seeking data, suddenly discovered himself to be alone. Since the workshift ended at five o'clock and it was only a little after three-thirty, it occurred to him that the absence of everyone else from the floor might have some significance. Guided by a murmur of voices, the research assistant made his way toward a lunchroom at the rear of the shop. He entered the lunch-room, and there they all were, the workers. Some of them were playing cards, some were reading, and some, I'm sure, since there was a healthy mix of men and women in the factory, were engaging in a bit of bantering and maybe even moving toward a little romance. One woman was reported to have been knitting a sweater.

In honest confusion the young research assistant asked the man nearest to him what was happening. Why weren't they all out at their benches working? "We've given them their money's worth," the man answered. "We've put together all the telephones we're going to make today."

As a worker, I dislike this story, as has every other worker I have ever told it to. Our dislike comes not only from being reduced to objects, specimens for study, but also from having our knowledge confirmed once again that to people concerned with, but not participating in, the work scene, we are merely part of the production process. Like the tools and machinery around us, we are items to be manipulated and used. In the years since this primitive study, all industries have developed enormous and sophis-ticated personnel departments, and although these early mistakes certainly are not duplicated, by and large this atti-tude has remained unchanged.

I first heard this story from what, unfortunately, almost every worker I have ever known regards with suspicion, a member of the academy, a college professor. (When some-one shows up on your work scene now, with no clear job to do, you know he's sure as hell not on your side.) In this instance the academic was merely being patronizing. He delivered the last line with a smile that said, "Those work-ers, don't forget they're rather a sharp lot of creatures, after all!" We are akin to the crafty peasant one finds often in French and Russian literature of the nineteenth century. Of course, one of the main points of his story was that the joke was on the sociologists and psychologists—it took so long to find us out. It is a cautionary tale, and the good professor was warning his students not to make the same mistake as those conducting the study. But there are other lessons to be learned from this story, and even though it has over the years been milked for all that it is worth, I would like to submit one or two more observations.

Among the questions that immediately come to a worker's mind is: how did the study team get away with all that wasted time for as long as they did? That kind of incompetency sure as hell wouldn't be tolerated for very long where I work. However, the point that the story makes best is that mankind cannot be studied in the abstract, and certainly not by means of different-colored lights and changing music. The study of man has to be the study of human beings.

It took the dozen or so scientists employed in that research effort almost two years to discover the absurdity of their study simply because in all that time none of them remained at work much later than three o'clock in the afternoon. But the factor that prolonged their mistake was that none of the research people connected their personal work habits to their job, the research project. Apparently none of them ever asked themselves why *they* quit early. Perhaps it was that in their striving for objectivity they refused to let their own feelings and emotions—their humanity—get involved in their work. Indeed, they very carefully, and apparently successfully, strove to keep it out. Among my acquaintances there are some university people. Although I do not know any who knit, many of them play cards, all of them read, and I guess I have seen at least a few of them make passes at each other, even on the job.

Their reasons for not being there were the same as the reasons of the subjects of their study, the workers, but it somehow escaped them that the workers might also have grown weary of what they were doing and wanted to call it a day. Unlike the workers under scrutiny, they did not have to stick around and punch a time clock, an infernal machine if ever there was one. They were at liberty to take off, leave early, and avoid the heavy crowds on the way home, perhaps, or just go do something else. Rubbing shoulders with the scientists on the floor of the factory, up until midafternoon anyway, were creatures that somewhat resembled themselves. Although dressed differently, they made noises similar to their own when surprised or frightened and they possessed appendages which they also called arms and legs. Hair, likewise, grew out of that portion of their anatomy which stood farthest from the earth. But they and the workers could not really have been of the same species. To the social scientists, the workers had to be alien creatures. Otherwise it would not have taken well over a year of research to find out something that they would have known immediately if they had looked inward to see how they themselves felt toward the end of the day.

It could be argued that someone was shortchanged in this episode I describe. The bosses were paying for eight hours and getting only six and a half or seven hours work. Speaking for the workers, I do not think so. They had accepted a quota that management had found profitable over the years, and they had filled that quota. I am not suggesting that those research assistants over the course of the study faked their notes to cover their time after three-thirty in the afternoon, although that may occasionally have happened. What I am arguing is that both sets of workers had pretty much achieved the six-and-a-half-hour day. Except that there was a distinct difference in the two groups. The workers, even after having struggled and pried loose from a tough and powerful employer a shorter work day, felt compelled to conceal what was an unquestionable labor gain. The other group, however, had the freedom of status to openly assume it as their prerequisite, their right.

I have never worked in a telephone assembly plant, but I have worked in similar light industry, and even from what little is revealed in this account, I know something about the factory in the Midwest. To begin with it was probably a pretty good place in which to work—at least it was then, when the study was conducted. It was good mainly because the workers were not at the complete mercy of their bosses and the production process. This in turn probably resulted in fairly good wages and conditions all around. Nothing spectacular, I would guess, but better than a lot of places I can think of. This could have been due to a strong trade union, but probably only partly so. I have worked as a member of one trade union or another all my life, and at times I have witnessed both wages and working conditions deteriorate, so it *can* happen. Workers, like everyone else, will use whatever means they have available to better themselves. In this instance, that of their improved working conditions, their union was not party to their gain. I do not think it is a mistake to say that what those people had, they got for themselves right there on the factory floor, by a very subtle process of insuring production results, a quota, if you will, in trade for control of their workday.

Beyond that I know very little about that factory, but

to a worker, good wages and a bit of control over his conditions at work are just about all he can hope for. Unquestionably there were some hard, dirty, disagreeable jobs in
that factory. Wherever you have punch presses you find
a lot of noise, and sharp metal edges to cut yourself on.
Telephones are probably packed about two dozen to a car-
ton, so somebody out on the loading dock would have
been doing some heavy lifting. However, what an assembly worker has to fight most is weariness and boredom.
After you have screwed a wire into its clip for about the
tenth time, the operation loses much of its fun and interest,
and you still have the day to get through. And a lifetime.

A positive side of their job, though, was that it was
social; most of the workers worked close enough together
so that they could talk to each other. Another good feature
was that there were men and women working together.
As far as I am concerned, at work or wherever, I like to
have women around, and so does most every other male I
have ever known. Practically all the women I know feel
the same way about the presence of men. Unquestionably
there were departments in that factory where women were
not present, probably where the heaviest work was being
done. I hope the men there were not too isolated. For centuries no one talked about it much, and longshoremen,
seamen, and many other workingmen rarely even thought
about it because it was all they had ever known, but to be
segregated from the opposite sex for the biggest and best
part of the day, every day you work, is not only unnatural
but unnecessary. I know of no work situation that has not
been integrated to the profit of both workers and management.

All things considered, then, most departments in that
communications factory were probably not bad places in

which to work. Compared to the situation in other plants, the workers had a lot going for them: good wages, good conditions, and a mixture of ages and sexes not unlike the world outside.

So, to those people who favor the underdog, we appear to have a happy ending here—stolid workers winning out over the bosses and science. Regrettably, since I did not work there, I cannot say whether it really ended happily or not. But work never ends, and there is no written record of what higher management, the top bosses, did after they found out about the early quits.

There is, however, a record of another department in that factory that I find interesting. The work scene was smaller—six women employed in wiring the circuit banks of telephone switchboards. The men leaning over their shoulders conducting the study discovered that no matter what they did, production went up. Good light, bad light, music, silence, no matter what the men did, short of beating those six women over their heads, production went up. After several months it was concluded, and I think rightly, that the rise in production was due to the study itself. Previously ignored, the women were pleased at the attention they were getting and sought to express their gratitude in the only way they knew, by working faster and more accurately. There is no record, however, of what happened when the study was terminated, the men suddenly withdrawn, and the six women left alone again with their new production quotas.

CHAPTER FOUR

Too Much Coffee Can Be Injurious to Your Health

Jesus Christ is supposed to have started out working as a carpenter. If he did, you could not prove it by me, because I have been through the source material and nowhere can I find any mention of his skill at putting a house together, or, for that matter, even working with wood. Of course, all that we know of him is from what others have said he told them. He may have talked about his work all the time and no one was sufficiently interested to write it down. "Now I remember once when I was starting out. We were working on this little duplex out north of town, and . . ." Listener (interrupting): "Yes, sir, Mr. Christ. Now, about where you say, 'Suffer not little children to come unto me,' and so forth. Do you mean *really* little kids, or preteenagers, too? Where is the cutoff age on that? Say about ten? Twelve?" Maybe nobody gave a damn.

If we know next to nothing about him, we know even less about the men he worked with, the other carpenters. Well, that was two thousand years ago, and things have a way of getting lost. However, if you live in a home constructed in the nineteenth century, you do not know very much more about the men who built it, either. You can go down into the cellar and look around, see how they joined the mud sill to the foundation or centered the joists exactly over the studs, but you really have no idea of what time the men who built your home went to work in the morning, got through at night, how much they earned, where *they* lived, what kind of life their wages permitted them to lead, or what they thought about it all. We know, or can find out, what Caesar had to say about Gaul and what Madame de Sévigné thought about Louis XIV, and pretty much how they spent their day. But nowhere is there recorded the lives and thoughts of those who dug their wells or tilled their fields. It is estimated that the ratio of royalty, aristocrats, and other ranks, that is, those down to and including gentry, to the rest of the population, the workers and peasants, was one to twenty in preindustrial Europe. Thus we know practically nothing about 95 percent of the western world's population for most of its history. Like gypsies and aborigines, workers have a history, with the exception of a few fragments, that goes back only as far as the recollections of the oldest living man or woman who happens to be around.

Setting aside one or two outstanding exceptions, the history of work and the people who did it exists hardly at all. When found, it is in scraps and pieces, trivia inadvertently dropped in corners and accidentally carried along in the heroic march of time made up of wars, dynasties, and long-dead leaders of defunct civilizations. A number of men and women have now recognized this loss and have turned back to retrieve it, the history of the overwhelming majority of mankind. Their work is more in the nature of archaeology than historical research, but is much harder than putting back together a Greek vase found shattered under some ancient wall. They do not even know if the pieces are all there. More accurately, they know that they probably are not. Even if they do find, through care, patience, curiosity, and hard digging, all the pieces in one particular instance and put, say, a vase back together again, they still have less than half of its story. If the master potter's mark is pressed into the bottom of the vase, it is a help, but he may have employed dozens of men under him. But then one day perhaps a thumbprint is discovered, baked into the underside of the curl of the spout, and then the true loss is brought home. What does one know really of the humanity of the man who made the container, not to mention the person, probably a woman, who carried it, heavy and dripping, back and forth from the well?

The unfortunate fact is that although mankind has a past, only a very small portion of it has been remembered and the rest of our history is lost forever. Today other forces are coming to bear, focusing especially on work, that will bury our past even more rapidly. Automation, different use of machinery, and changing work practices are eliminating jobs so quickly that the way I made my living only a dozen years ago is as unknown to a youngster now entering the workforce as that ancient carpenter's two millennia ago.

For a century the coffee of the world has been shipped to market as green beans inside burlap sacks. Brazilian coffee, called Santos, used to be unique in that it was put up in 132-pound bags, but now they have conformed, and their stuff weighs the same as all the other coffee coming in from Central and South America, 154 pounds or 70 kilos. The sacks of the coffee that arrives here from Africa weigh the same. One used to encounter small, odd lots from strange places in 100-pound sacks, but that was many years ago, and I do not know what happened to that "light" coffee. Also, until recently, sacks in from Indonesia traditionally weighed 200 pounds, and were like great, rigid tubes, the beans were so tightly packed inside them. These sacks also had very small ears, leaving you not very much to grab on to when you lifted them. However, the Indonesians reduced the size of their sacks, thank God, and eventually it came in a variety of shapes and weights; in addition to the standard 154 pounds, I worked sacks from there weighing 110, 120, and 132 pounds. Once even 88 pounds. I have no idea why they could not make up their minds.

Traditionally, coffee was discharged from the holds of ships in rope slings. Down there where the coffee was stowed we would lay out a closed loop of manila rope on top of the sacks and start loading the sling. Twelve sacks, in three piles four high, constituted a load. We then threaded one end of the rope loop through the other "eye" so it would cinch itself tight when the hook took the weight. After giving a signal to the winch driver, we would step back, and away the load would go. When you knew what you were doing, it was not all that bad of a job. You were never lifting sacks up more than about waist high. After you had dug down you could usually use low sacks for the bottom if you planned ahead and, reaching back, find something higher up to top off the load. Discharging coffee was never easy, but after you learned your way around it you could do the work almost unconsciously, keeping a conversation going with your partner except when you actually lifted the sacks. That is, if you could find all that much to talk about for eight or ten hours at a stretch. A coffee job had other compensations, too. I guess sacks are just about the nicest cargo to stretch out on top of for five minutes if the winches break down, or if you just manage to get ahead of the game.

Out on the dock the sling load of coffee was landed onto a low, sturdy cart called a four-wheeler which was dragged around from pile to pile by two dockmen, who threw the sacks off the cart and sorted them by marks or numbers stenciled on the end of each sack. On the West Coast the normal gang size was six men in the hold of the ship and eight men on the dock, meaning three teams working against four. Sometimes the ship you were working would have a lot of different marks, maybe fifteen or twenty. Sometimes it would have only a few, maybe only one or two. If there were a lot of marks it was to the advantage of the men working in the hold; very few marks gave the dockmen an edge. This was because if in a load of twelve sacks of coffee there were, say, twelve different marks, the men with four-wheelers on the dock had to pull the coffee around to twelve different locations to throw off their sacks. Even with rotation, that meant by the time they were through with one sling load, there was another waiting for them, hanging on the hook. If there were only a few marks it meant they could throw off their load in a hurry and sit down. A four-wheeler is not as comfortable to sit down on as the coffee sacks in the hold of the ship, but it is better than not sitting down at all.

Longshoremen, like everybody else in the world, like to sit down a lot. When I first came on the waterfront, one of my first jobs was working coffee on the dock. My partner was a black man with a big belly who was getting along in years. When we turned to that morning the gangs on the ship had to rig the booms and uncover the hatches, so we had a little time before we got our first load. My partner spent that time searching around collecting two-by-fours and other scraps of lumber. Finally I got tired of watching him and asked him what he was doing. He did not reply at first, but busied himself with poking the lumber into a stack of pallet boards just inside the door of the shed, beside the ship. Finally he had four two-by-fours sticking out at a convenient height above the floor, and he turned around and sat down on them. He had two one-by-eights protruding out on either side of him, a little higher than the two-by-fours, for arm rests. His fingers were laced together across the front of him, comfortably holding up his big belly.

"Son, you haven't been down here very long, have you?" he said, looking at me speculatively.

"No, I haven't," I acknowledged.

"Well, boy, I'm going to tell you how to get along on this waterfront. When you come to work in the morning, the first thing you do is you construct yourself a good seat. And the second thing you do is make sure you use it a lot."

In this world, sometimes the best of advice just drops in your lap.

But that day there were a lot of marks, I remember, and the old man got to use his seat hardly at all. By five o'clock we were both dragging ass.

All this was changed several years later. At the time, longshoremen questioned whether it was for the better. We no longer had dock men sorting coffee on the pier. They were eliminated. Instead of using rope slings, we sent pallet boards directly into the hatch. We loaded them with coffee down there in the hold, twelve sacks to a board and sometimes more. All of the sacks on a pallet board had to be of the same mark, so the sorting was done in the hold of the ship, too. This change in the operation made a considerable difference in how the coffee was worked.

Formerly we made up our sling loads of sacks without regard to where the coffee was stowed, even in the far, dark corners of the hold. We hooked up the load back there, and the winch driver dragged the coffee out to the square of the hatch for us, lifted it up, and took it away. However, a pallet board cannot be dragged over sacks of coffee—it rips the hell out of them. Nevertheless, a pallet board had to be taken back into the corners of the hold where the coffee was stowed. After the board was loaded, it had to be brought back out to the square opening of the hatch so that the hook could lift it straight up and take it away. This was all done, physically, by the longshoremen.

In some ports they used two greased planks for a runway for the pallet boards. In other ports they used eight-foot lengths of heavy steel rollers, strung together, to get the pallet boards back to where the coffee was. Even if you had a choice between the two, neither was very attractive. Since you cannot push a loaded pallet board with a ton of coffee on it uphill, it was essential to build in a slight slope as the runway went back into the hold—so that you were going downhill when you pushed the board back out loaded. Pushing downhill was usually no problem with rollers; once you got the load moving, you could even jump on top of the coffee sacks for a ride.

Unfortunately, there was a drawback. In order to go downhill you had to build a hill to go down, so you started out high up way back in the hold. The empty pallet board, when you began loading it, was already somewhere above your knees, and you started by stacking the sacks on top of it from there, ending up about head high. Since the coffee was also being sorted on the ship, you were constantly skimming off to get the same mark. Most of the sacks you lifted came from down around your feet. Bend down, grab on to a sack, and then lift the whole 154 pounds of it all the way up and over. What all this meant was that when a coffee ship came into port you did not see longshoremen pushing each other aside to get at those jobs.

Why was coffee sorted directly on the ship? It cut out eight men from the operation, they were no longer on the payroll, and the stevedore company saved money. This new procedure for working coffee was initiated under a new clause in the union contract permitting change through automation, of all things, by union officials who did not have to work the coffee, of course.

Since longshoremen have a reputation for labor militancy (nobody pushes *us* around. Oh yeah?) it remained a mystery outside the industry why these workers agreed to this innovation. Discharging coffee became godawful harder than it had been, and it had never been a vacation. So what happened? The answer is found in the politics of work itself, and it still makes many of the older, retired longshoremen uncomfortable.

The nature of the work changed only for the men who actually handled the sacks and lifted the weight. The winch driver's job remained the same; he went on manipulating his handles up and down. The gang boss made out the same old time sheet and went home early. The forklift driver continued to raise his blades and pick up the load, and the cargo checker counted the sacks the same as always. If all these men, plus the car men, the hook-on men, the equipment men, and the mechanics, plus the pensioners, who also voted and who received a healthy increase under the contract that permitted this innovation, are added together, their numbers were found to be approximately twice that of the men in the hold of the ship doing the actual work. When the vote was taken on the contract that permitted this change in work, it was discovered that it carried by a ratio of approximately two to one.

I know of more than one longshore family in which relationships between father and son became strained over this agreement. If the moral of this story is not to let the power of the vote get away from where the hard work is, the working longshoremen took it to heart and disenfranchised the pensioners—they were denied a vote when the next contract came up for ratification—but the damage was already done. A few years later, the discharge of coffee was modified again. We opened a coffee hatch one morning and discovered that the coffee sacks were already stacked on pallet boards. After we cleared a space, a forklift was sent into the hold to pick up all the heavy coffee and bring it out into the square of the hatch to be lifted away. The hard work had been transferred down to Brazil or Central America somewhere. I do not know how our Latin brothers regarded this move, but we longshoremen in San Francisco were not altogether unhappy, even though it meant losing two more men from the hold. Everything ends up having a price.

Perhaps you have asked yourself why sacks are made to hold 154 pounds of coffee. Why 154, why not less? It has to do with calculus, and with the absolute maximum weight that average men can repeatedly handle over a day's time. One hundred and fifty-four pounds is about tops. (In San Francisco, coffee is thrown two men to a sack, but down there where it is grown, one man handles it all alone; carrying it on his shoulders, he walks the sack back into the hold of the ship and drops it in place.) Unquestionably, really big, well-built men could handle more weight. But a quick look around you will tell you that such men are in the minority, and if you are going to get your coffee loaded anywhere in the world, you have to deal with averages. Otherwise, somebody might stagger.

The calculus comes in because of the price of the burlap sacking. Simple mathematics instructs us that the most efficient container is a sphere. It surrounds the most volume for the least outward surface area, and any container tending toward a sphere, or a ball, tends to be more efficient. It is also a law of mathematics that a large ball has proportionately more volume to surface area than a small one. That is, a large orange has less peel than two small oranges each weighing exactly half as much. Sacks of coffee are not spherical, but they tend in that direction. Two 77-pound sacks of coffee would use approximately 15 percent more burlap than one sack weighing 154 pounds. Hence the reason behind the size and weight of a sack of coffee. The small piece of burlap that is saved on every sack probably only costs a few pennies, but every little bit counts, and it all mounts up when somebody is out to make a buck.

The bottom line, profit, has an inordinate command over work and the individual worker. The great industrial heartland of America, from Pennsylvania west through Ohio, Michigan, Indiana, and Illinois, was in a very brief time turned into the rust belt, not because the raw materials, coal and iron, gave out, or because the factories and skilled workers disappeared, but because those controlling the means of production could get it done cheaper somewhere else. But the cost of industrial labor has a way of leveling itself out in the industrial world. What is cheap labor today usually turns out to be equal in cost tomorrow; witness Germany's and Japan's labor costs now as opposed to merely ten years ago. Still, however brief in the vast span of history, those few years, seen in human terms, mean mass unemployment, poverty, and futures without hope for those workers and their families who live there.

The rust belt may eventually recover. New products and new factories to produce them may eventually return to the Midwest. Those workers presently unemployed there might once again return to the living world. If they do, however, the workers will have had nothing to do with being put back to work. It will have been an economic decision, made by people seizing an opportunity for profit, people whom the workers very likely will never know and who will never know them. Meanwhile the workers merely exist, in place, waiting to be employed once more by some unknown group who, when they finally appear, will unquestionably present themselves as benefactors.

When work disappears, workers always regret its loss. If it was hard work, the loss may be easier to accept, but we would all rather have hard work than no work at all. Coffee, now discharged in the ports of America already palletized, is once again in the process of change. Seagoing vans loaded with coffee are beginning to make an appearance. Soon it will be unnecessary for any longshoreman even to touch the cargo. We are happy to put away our sack hooks and discontinue doing that hard work. On the other hand, more than two-thirds fewer of us are now employed than formerly in that discharge operation. Now as longshoremen retire they are not being replaced. This is happening in industry all over America, creating the equivalent of little rust belts everywhere.

When a work process goes through radical change,

employers cut manpower to the bone, their theory being that they can always add more workers if they have to. And if they do add people, they do it grudgingly. Sometimes they will refuse even when there is an obvious need to employ more workers. If the product takes a beating, so be it. Pass on the losses to the next entrepreneur up the line, or hope to write it off as an insurance claim.

When the first coffee came into our port already palletized, I was driving a forklift on the dock. Two hook-on men landed the load, and I took it away and stacked it inside the pier. Although there were other gangs working, there were only three men to a hatch. Since the loads were a jumble because of the ship's rolling action on the voyage north, sacks of coffee fell off the pallet board with every movement of my forklift no matter how carefully I maneuvered it. At first the hook-on men and I dragged the sacks aside so I could get through to the pile. After a while we quit doing that, because, first, there were just too many sacks of coffee scattered about the floor of the dock, and second, it was not our job. I lowered the blades of the lift to the floor and turned off the motor, and the three of us waited. It took about five minutes for the walking boss to show up.

"What's happening?" the walking boss asked me. He had a young superintendent in tow who appeared slightly nervous.

"There's too much coffee on the floor," I said. "I can't get through to the pile. You need to get a couple of men from the hiring hall to clean up." The walking boss motioned to the hook-on men.

"Hey, Willie," he said. "You and Ollie come over here. I want you to drag these sacks out of the way." Willie shook his head.

"No way," Ollie said, folding his gloves and slipping them into his hip pocket. "We are the *hook men*. We don't do nothin' else."

"I can fire you for not working as directed," the walking boss threatened. Willie and Ollie looked glumly down at their shoes and reached around for their jackets, preparing to go home.

"If you force the hook-on men to deal with that coffee," I said, "this gang will be down. There won't be any more coffee coming out of this hatch." We were talking five men in the hold, two winch drivers, and a gang boss— eight men, counting myself. It was the walking boss's turn to stare glumly at his shoes.

"We need two more men from the hall," he stated decisively to the superintendent and headed for the telephone.

We got the two more men from the hall, but, since there were four gangs discharging coffee, the new men were very shortly swamped with work. I and the other gang forklift drivers had to wait our turn for our aisles to be cleared of fallen sacks of coffee. The hooks were hanging and production was suffering. Very soon the walking boss was by my side again.

"Can you put an empty pallet board on your blades and just kind of shove these fallen sacks aside?" he asked.

"If I do that, it's going to rip the hell out of a lot of the sacks," I replied. "You're going to have loose coffee beans all over this dock. You know that."

The walking boss shook his head, thinking about all that lost coffee that would have to be shoveled into the Bay.

"Go ahead," he said. "Shove it aside. The superintendent says they won't let him hire any more men. Shove it out of the way and keep going."

I can refuse to work, legally, according to our longshore

agreement, if my health or safety is threatened. It is in our contract. But I cannot refuse to work merely to protect cargo. I shoved a lot of coffee aside, as carefully as I knew how, for the rest of the workday. But I still tore up a lot of sacks. By the time the shift was over, there were a good dozen sacks scattered around, ripped open, with many hundreds of pounds of coffee destroyed. The three other gang drivers had done about the same. At eighty cents a pound, dockside, they could have hired ample men to pick up those sacks and still saved money. But they, the stevedore company, chose not to. They passed the loss on to somewhere else, either back to the ship, to the coffee wholesaler, or to some insurance company. Ultimately, of course, to the consumer.

When the coffee began arriving in the containers, closed vans, another problem developed. The coffee was loaded in the heat of the tropics, and when the ship reached the cool West Coast, the coffee began to sweat. Taking on moisture, the green beans became wet and worthless, especially the top layer of sacks in each van. We were confronted with the sight of containers parked all over the docks with their doors open, drying out. Much of the coffee was lost, as much as 15 percent, I learned later. A terrible waste, but a waste still deemed viable by the coffee industry, at least in America, evidently.

No one likes to see his work wasted. Coffee beans are still picked by hand, one by one, a bean at a time, in Brazil, Colombia, or wherever. There are thousands upon thousands upon thousands of coffee beans in a 154-pound sack. One wonders what Juan Valdez would think about it all, down there in the tropics, seeing the product of several weeks of his work destroyed almost in an instant by a forklift driver in Frisco.

CHAPTER FIVE

Oh, to Be Free Again!

Small-craft fishermen are reputed to like their work, and with few exceptions all the fishermen I ever met did it by choice. Even with all the cold and the wetness, most of them stick with it instead of going into another line of work. The same goes for cabinetmakers; with them we can explain it because they are fashioning something from raw material, with their hands, and when they are finished there is something new in the world that is useful and beautiful and that they have themselves made. As for fishermen, for all I know they may be satisfying some primeval urge, what with the sea and all the mystery that surrounds it. Besides, it is always rewarding to get something from nature that is good to eat.

Assembly-line workers do not like their work, and these two occupations, fishing and cabinetmaking, are the ones most often named when you ask male assembly-line workers what, of all jobs, they would most like to do for a living. If he is a native to the Midwest, the factory worker may never have seen the ocean, much less a fishing boat, and he knows in the back of his mind that if he made furniture for a living, instead of running a hand plane down a straight, dry piece of wood in a nice clean basement and feeling the crisp, sweet-smelling shavings curl up over his fingers, he undoubtedly would be on another assembly line in North Carolina or Grand Rapids. Probably for less money.

Driving truck is the third most common alternative occupation mentioned, after going fishing or making things out of wood. When driving truck is given as a desirable alternative occupation it is a more serious and studied reply, because driving truck is possible. It is all around us.

Choice, control, and decision-making in their work are three advantages that truck drivers, to the uninitiated, appear to have to a degree greater than almost any other category of blue collar workers in this country. That is why there are so many truck drivers, real and would-be, in America. And the burning desire of men to make their living while enjoying these advantages has now resulted in these very advantages being used against the men who drive truck for a living.

I decided once many years ago that I might like to drive a truck, and even took some preliminary steps to make my living that way. Since I knew a number of truck drivers, I thought I was not as uninformed about the job as most men. If you had asked me what truck drivers did all day long, other than count telephone poles, I felt I could have replied with some accuracy and enthusiasm. It is hard work, I would have said, and a responsible job—all that equipment. But isn't that what a man wants? I even thought I could describe myself going through a typical day. When I first cranked the motor over in the morning before I took the rig out to pick up the load, I'd listen carefully to hear if everything was all right. Is that a knock? Nooo . . . that's just a valve tappet rapping away. It'll disappear once the motor warms up.

I was also realistic. I would start out working for someone else, I figured, and owning my own rig someday was only a thought far off in the back of my mind. But even working for someone else, when I pulled that rig away from the barn in the morning I would leave the boss and all other supervision behind. I would not have to put up with *that* crap anymore. I would be on my own, and that is the way I wanted it.

I was aware that getting a big tractor and semitrailer out of a city is a serious undertaking. Every start and stop means going up through a lot of gears to gather momentum. Furthermore, though moving a load over the road is the truck driver's livelihood, people in cars seem to regard trucks as merely unpleasant obstacles to be darted around and cut off from progress. But I could handle that with skill and forbearance. It was going to be part of my job, and I would not even get mad at those people.

Traffic changes daily, and so does the weather, and once on the road I would be free to check on the progress of new buildings being constructed, new signs being put up, and whether or not it was going to remain sunny or rain before evening. Out in the country I could watch the crops being tilled and the leaves drop in the fall and come out again in the spring.

There were drawbacks to the job, I knew. A truck driver works alone, and I am not all that much of a loner. With no other workers around to express approval, no one, except those anonymous motorists I passed on the highway, would ever have a chance to find out what a hell of a good driver I *was*. But there would be the camaraderie of the road. Before long I would know all the other drivers on the run, the color, size, and make of their rigs, how many horsepower they had, and who they had worked for last. Every time I passed someone I knew we would give a blast of the horn and wave at each other. Where would I meet them and how would I get to know the other drivers? During the lunch and coffee stops where truckers gathered, of course.

Years ago, many roadside restaurants built up a reputation for good food through having a lot of trucks parked out front, the theory being that no one knew the road better than the truck driver. Sooner or later, everyone came to realize that there was something wrong with this reasoning, because the food was so often bad. What the average motorist did not understand was that most truck drivers do not stop at any given restaurant for the food but to see other truck drivers. I wasn't going to be any different. To hell with the food, I was going to be one of the guys—probably I would even kid the waitress, even though that is not my style. I had no plans to haul coast to coast, or even make the San Francisco–to–L.A. run, except now and then for a change, and so when I came home every evening and my wife asked, "How'd it go today, honey?" and I replied, "Oh, about the same as yesterday," it would not mean that I disliked my work.

I got my first hint of what a truck driver's life was really like when I began inquiring around for a job. There weren't any. I had made a few runs with friends who had let me drive a bit out on the highway to gain road time, and I also had had some experience docking a rig—backing up the trailer to a warehouse door or loading platform. This is the most difficult chore in driving, since you usually have only a few inches of clearance on either side of the van and you have to end up square with the dock and, frequently, with the tractor jackknifed around so that it does not block traffic. Anyway, I was ready, I felt, to kick over my motor and make my first haul. And then I couldn't find a motor to kick over.

All of the trucking concerns where I asked for a job not only had a waiting list of experienced drivers, but were laying off men. The only man who had a chance of going to work under those conditions was a brother-in-law. Finally, a man I knew, a dispatcher for a trucking outfit, set me straight. "If you really want to drive truck for a living," he said, "why don't you buy your own rig? I'll put you in touch with a freight broker I know, and you'll be on your way."

"Are you telling me it's easier to start out owning your own business than it is to work up to it?" I asked.

"That's the way it is in trucking," he replied. "It's the trend."

A new diesel tractor costs three or four times as much as the driver's annual wage, though they are easier to buy and probably take a smaller down payment than a modern home. Most long-haul trucking today is done by independent operators, men who own their own rigs. There have always been wildcat operators, but up until a decade or so ago most freight was handled by the manufacturers, using their own equipment, or they turned it over to large trucking concerns that hauled it on contract. The independent trucker handled the odd lots and the slop-over. Very quickly the manufacturers and freight forwarders around our larger cities discovered they were getting their odd lots and slop-over hauled cheaper. It may have cost them a trifle more on a tonnage basis, but they more than made this back if they simply stopped using their own trucks and turned it all over to the independents, because then they did not have to purchase and maintain their own equipment.

Or hire their own drivers. Whatever you care to say against it, the International Brotherhood of Teamsters has got its people vacations, pensions, and medical benefits. The independent truck driver gives up all of these to make himself more competitive. Fringe benefits now cost an employer almost half as much per hour as the worker's hourly wage. Manufacturers know a good thing when they see it, and those companies that could manage to do so have turned all their trucking over to the independent operators.

Just as in our southern states a generation or two ago the longing to get away from looking over a plow at a mule's ass all day long as it plodded down a furrow sent a lot of farm boys north, so now the desperate desire to escape the assembly line has led a lot of their sons to scrape a few dollars together and buy a truck. In a sense, the man who does this is buying himself a job, but only he can tell you how expensive it becomes. For openers, he has to foot the bill for maintenance on his equipment—it is his truck, after all, and he will be out of work if it breaks down. In addition, he forgoes vacations and retirement, sees his family only occasionally at odd hours, denies himself time off even if he is sick, lets his teeth rot, and promises delivery over the weekend while working through Sunday for the equivalent of straight time wages. It is a high price to pay for the pleasure of gabbing back and forth over a citizens band radio. Ten-four, ol' buddy.

To keep his head above water an independent trucker has to drive and drive and drive. He has to keep that rig moving. The truck may remain idle, but the payments on it keep coming due. Unless he has a solid freight connection somewhere and can hustle his own cargo, the independent can get a load only by paying a 15 percent fee to a freight broker. This is 15 percent of his gross payment for hauling the load—it comes right off the top. Insurance on a truck costs ten times as much as it does for your family sedan. (The only insurance any truck driver I know has is on his truck; certainly he has none on himself.) Each one of those eighteen tires rolling beneath him costs well over two hundred dollars. You might be able to buy a replacement motor for your Chevy for fifteen hundred dollars or so, but a short-block overhaul on a diesel engine can cost five times that much. Pressed in by all these costs, the independent trucker responds by pushing himself harder, taking longer hauls and more freight for essentially less money. Most states have a 76,000-pound load limit for a truck's gross weight. There are scales placed at strategic points to enforce that limit, and fines are levied for excess tonnage. But the overweight becomes just about the trucker's entire margin of profit. In many states in America the scales still close at midnight. Out of sight around a bend in the road one can observe lines of trucks pulled over to the side waiting. They start revving up their motors about twelve-fifteen.

The squeeze the trucker finds himself caught in, like most of the pressures of the world, comes on gradually, and the trucker's traditional response is to bear down harder—on himself. Every now and then, however, something happens to upset the equilibrium. The fuel crises of recent years have, on occasion, almost brought things to a standstill. When diesel fuel suddenly jumps ten cents a gallon overnight, truckers frequently cannot move; it actually *costs* them money to drive. The brokers and manufacturers have no control over *that*. The income and profits of the brokers and the manufacturers have had to be cut back at times just to get the trucks moving again. Blame it all on the oil companies and the Arabs. Recently some independent truckers have rebelled and begun to organize themselves. What the long-term effect of their effort will be is still unknown.

One wonders why the truckers keep plugging away at it. (I never did drive truck for a living. When the day came to take the driving test for my Class A chauffeur's license, I didn't bother to show up for the examination.) A while back I asked a truck driver friend of mine, an independent operator, why he did not quit. Just give up and quit. He had recently, a mutual friend told me, taken a load of lettuce from the Mexican border straight through to Seattle. He had stopped only to take a leak, fuel up, and grab a cheeseburger (to be eaten on the road). Arriving in Seattle exhausted in the middle of the night, he had fallen asleep over the wheel. When someone woke him up six hours later, his motor was still running.

"Why do I keep doing it?" he said. "Well, bad as it is, it still beats working on an assembly line."

CHAPTER SIX

Old Blue Collars, Young Blue Collars, and That Little Place You're Going to Get in the Country

"Kids don't want to work nowadays." I hear this statement made every day I work. Naturally, it is made by some old-timer. I think it is generally true, but I have mixed feelings about it. In the first place, why the hell should they? Why should anyone want to harness himself all day long to something that is hard, or monotonous, or dirty, and frequently all three? The statement has probably always been with us, voiced over the centuries by older workers since God knows when. On the other hand, nothing comes free in the world, and if you aren't carrying your own weight it simply means that someone else is packing it for you. The old-timer has a point here. Why should it be him?

Leaving aside the man with a work ethic— that is, the type of guy who works hard because he thinks hard work is virtuous and he feels good only when is he tired—there really isn't much to argue about here between the old-timer and the kid. When an old-timer says of some younger man that he doesn't want to work, he is usually complaining that the kid hasn't picked up *his* work habits yet. Who needs them, maybe. But if the kid really isn't doing enough work, that is an argument that should probably take place between the kid and the man who signs his checks.

Of course, this does not hold true if the kid and the old-timer are working at some job together and the kid is not doing his share, or the kid has contrived things so that the old-timer is doing more than he is. Then the old-timer has a legitimate complaint. For instance, suppose that the two of them are throwing coffee together, one on each end of the sack, and the kid is taking a slight jump on his partner and lifting up his end first, putting the bulk of the coffee beans, and the weight, down at the old-timer's end of the sack—a practice known as giving someone "the Portagee Lift." In a situation like this, I am on the side of the old-timer. But most kids won't do this. At least not more than once. There is a countermove to the Portagee Lift known as "the Dago Stall." (In northern Europe I am sure there are equally insulting terms featuring Finns and Swedes.) Moves and countermoves can get very involved, and if the situation goes on long enough it will usually end up with a series called the left jab and the right cross. The best solution is to separate the team before it goes this far and give the kid a new partner who works just like him. Then everyone can be entertained watching them work against each other all day long.

But young workers do approach labor differently from old workers. I have worked with black men, orientals, Latinos, and just about every European ethnic group found in America; inside the work scene itself, if there is a split, it is as pronounced along generational lines as any other. The slow loss of vitality that takes place over the years is certainly a factor that bonds older workers together, but it is insufficient as an explanation if you consider the lively old men you encounter here and there. They are more likely to share the attitudes of their own age group than those of the lively young.

As I grow older, I have noticed in myself and in the older men I work with an acceptance that it is easier to *do* the job than to fight it. As you grow older working, work becomes your "thing," and you do it with somewhat less resistance. When they are young and first go to work, most people, especially if they are white and they live in America, do not accept work as their fate. If they aren't angling to rise to a boss's job, then they frequently have some scheme in the backs of their heads to start a business for themselves, however small, or buy a little farm in the country. Some of them make it. Most do not. The man who starts a small business invariably finds that he is working about eighteen hours a day for the same income he made back at the factory working eight. The worker who becomes a small farmer usually ends up even worse off, since agro-economics is not learned working on the assembly line.

Years ago, chicken ranches were popular, and I know several men who ventured in that direction. "What happened?" I asked one would-be chicken farmer I knew who showed up on the job after an absence of a few years.

"Feed," he said. "It cost more to feed them than they were worth."

This was literally true. Being a small operator he was unable to buy feed in large tonnage lots and had to pay top price for it. Although he was getting thirty-six cents a pound for his fryers, it was costing him forty cents a pound to bring them to market. Even though he kept track of costs, economic reality wasn't brought home to him until one day a virus swept his flock when it was young and all the little chicks died. He "made" more money, as he put it, off that batch of birds than any other.

His wife had worked at the telephone company all during this time to keep their heads above water. She had pitched right in, working Mondays through Fridays in town and then helping to clean out the chicken pens on the weekend. After they quit raising chickens, she kept her job. Now that they were both making wages they were fairly well off, and I had expected them to be enjoying their new affluence. But I was wrong. He was still driving the same old banged-up pickup truck.

"When you going to get a new car?" a mutual friend asked him. The three of us were eating lunch.

"No way," the former chicken rancher said, shaking his head and biting into a peanut butter sandwich. "We're saving our money."

"What for?" I asked.

"Calves."

"What?"

"I can buy drop calves from the dairies for fifteen bucks apiece," he explained. "Soon as we save enough money, I'm quitting my job and we're going to raise beef. Sell them as yearlings. There's a lot of money in it."

"What about feed?" I asked.

"I've looked into that. They eat mostly hay."

"What does your wife think of it?" the other man asked him.

"She's all for it," he replied with enthusiasm. "She's

happy about it. She'll go for anything to get away from all that chickenshit."

She may have gotten away from *some* of that chicken-shit, as the other man observed later, but she wasn't getting away from all of it. To get away from *all* that chickenshit, she would have to get a divorce.

Although this would-be cattle baron was not young, his schemes are typical of those of a lot of young workers. It seems not to occur to them that the work they are doing now is the work they will be doing for the rest of their lives. It takes a while for that understanding to sink in. Sometimes it never does. Without the attitudes and values of a workingman, the man working is something else.

The one group of American workingmen who learned this earliest and know it most completely, it seems to me, are older blacks, especially if they are from the South. Given their start, it would be pretty foolish of them to look forward in life to anything but work. These men have taught me a lot when it comes to hard, physical labor. The work is going to be there tomorrow. But if *you* are important, what you do today is important, so do it right.

Black people are separated along generational lines just as much as any other group, and the gap takes the same form as with whites. But the civil rights movement has increased opportunities and has had a tremendous impact on young blacks. Blue-collar work is not the only course open to them anymore, and now they have their schemes too. Their dreams may not be of chicken ranches, but they are pretty much the equivalent. Furthermore, personal drive and ambition seem to me to be more pronounced among the young black workers that I know than among the white. The myth of the lazy black may persist in some quarters, but among those workers I know who are moonlighting at other jobs, blacks far outnumber whites. Not only does the black worker often work two jobs himself, but his wife is usually employed. Also, blacks are among the hardest hitters when it comes to going after overtime.

Curiously, the two groups of workers that are farthest apart in all other respects—young blacks and older whites—have one thing in common. When it comes to their kids, young blacks are ambitious as hell in the old-fashioned sense. They are just as high on education for their young as the older white workers ever were, and for the same reason—they think education will get their children away from manual labor and into white-collar work or the professions.

I do not know what the end result of this ambition will be in the young black worker, but in the older white man it has frequently left him disappointed and confused. If you work all your life but raise your kids to avoid it, you have made an obvious criticism of your own life spent working. If you are a trade unionist and along the way you have helped to raise the wages and working conditions of yourself and other working people, everything you have done in this direction you can be proud of. Without exception, all old-timers are. Still, they want their kids out of it, which means getting them into the white-collar middle class.

It is true that workers, older workers in particular, have extremely naive ideas of what white-collar people do for a living. They see them as going through life staying clean, sitting on their butts, and making a lot of money doing it. They also see them gaining a great deal of status and respect that they feel are denied them as blue-collar work-

ers. That is what they want for their kids. From listening
to the complaints of my white-collar friends, however, I
get the impression that though white-collar people may
stay clean and may spend much of their time sitting down,
they all seem to put in a pretty full, hard day. As for prestige, they may not be on the bottom of the totem pole, but
there is always someone above them, and if that person is
a petty tyrant the underdog is not protected by a trade
union. To cap it off, most of them make less money than
I do.

The fact that all white-collar workers are not enjoying a
picnic occasionally filters down to the ranks of blue-collar
workers, even if they have no white-collar friends. Many
years ago in San Francisco, the longshoremen opened their
ranks to take in six hundred new men, and there were
fourteen thousand applicants for those few hundred jobs.
Almost half of the applicants were schoolteachers, and a
big hunk of the remainder were in white-collar occupations. When I asked an older longshoreman, who had two
kids in college, what he made of this, he just shook his
head. His confusion left him with no response. White-collar people, apparently in large numbers, would eagerly
trade places with him. Maybe in the case of these white-
collar men it was simply an instance of the grass appearing
greener, but most older longshoremen I know would not
accept that explanation. This attitude is not as persistent
among the younger blue-collar workers; but among the
old-timers, the grass *has* to be greener over there in the
white-collar fields.

A lifetime of hard work and perhaps childhood memories of the depression combined to solidify the older blue-
collar worker's attitude. Poverty and hard work are twin
plagues; education is the vaccination against them, and, by

God, his kid is going to have one. Education is the one thing he did *not* have, so it must be the answer, he feels, and it is pretty hard to shake him out of it. And the kid had better not blow it, either. I once came upon an old winch driver, a father whose son had gone to work on the waterfront the same time as I had. The son was working below in the lower hold of the ship in the same gang as I was, palletizing two-hundred-pound sacks of coffee. The old man was so angry he was dancing up and down.

"Look at him," he said to me. "Look at him! He wouldn't have to be doing that. No! Goddammit, he could have gone to college! If he hadn't knocked up that little twist and had to get married, he could've gone to college."

As I looked down to where the work was being done, I did not know whom to sympathize with. It was very hard work. I knew because I had been doing it myself all day. I had come up on deck to take a leak, and now I was going back down below to throw coffee for a couple hours more. As I watched I realized the son was not merely tired, but in trouble. He was young and he had not done much of that kind of work, and as yet he was not very good at it. He and his partner were having to lift the sacks up almost head high to top off the load, and they were getting the coffee from down around their shoelaces. Both the son and his partner were just barely making it.

The old man understood. He had done a lot of hard work in his time and he knew what it was like. Over the years he had worked himself up to a job where all he had to do was manipulate a couple of handles up and down, and now, with rage and frustration, he was reliving all that hard work through watching his son do it, which was probably worse, to him anyway. Watching your son go through a cruel form of torture is cruel torture too, and I could sympathize, seeing it through the old man's eyes. Even more, it seemed a bitter punishment for someone whose crime, at the age of about nineteen, had been making love.

Finally, however, you always see things from where you are standing, and everything has a way of sorting itself out. On deck beside the old man I had to turn away so as not to witness his agony. Going down the ladder to the lower hold, however, my viewpoint changed. Perhaps I should not have said it, but I could not help myself.

"What about me, asshole?" I yelled up at him. "I've been to college, and it doesn't make those sacks any lighter."

I cherish old-timers, however. Most of what I know about work, the ways of the world, who the enemy is, I learned from old-timers. On your first day on a new job, it is usually an old-timer who makes the first overture of friendship. When you are a kid just starting out, it is a rare old-timer who won't show you the ropes, not just on how to get along on the job and how to do your work, but what the score is generally—what bars and saloons to stay away from, and so forth. I started out working as a kid in the late thirties, and my head is still full of information of this sort that I treasure. Although I never had occasion to put much of it to use and most of it is now obsolete, I will never forget it:

When you are on the bum, watch out for those tin cans you find under bridges. Don't step on them and smash them just for the hell of it. Guys cook *food* in those cans. And if you use a can yourself, leave it clean for the next guy. And be sure you dry it out good and turn it upside down so it doesn't get rusty.

Do not hobo through the southern states in the late

springtime. That is when they repair the flood damage, and you might end up on a road gang. Worse, next month the sheriff might pass you on to the next county and you are liable to spend all summer down there on the end of a long-handled shovel. However, they *will* let you go in the fall. If there is no work to be done, they don't want to feed you.

If you land in jail, don't accept any gift, not even a candy bar, from *anyone!* I haven't seen anyone roll a handmade cigarette in twenty years, and I don't smoke myself anymore, but I know that if you land in jail you're supposed to throw your Bull Durham into the common pot— usually a coffee can—with everybody else's tobacco. And you shouldn't hold out. That way not only will you show everyone that you're okay, but later on when you might not have any money left to buy tobacco yourself you will have established the right to dip into the common pot. Incidentally, if I take up smoking again and I am broke and getting toward the end of the pack, I will never smoke my last cigarette. That way I will never run out.

If you are sleeping in a park, or anywhere in or close to a city, don't take off your shoes. If they are any good, most likely they will be stolen. And no one is going anywhere without shoes.

Here's a really obsolete tip. If you're picking cotton, if you have no intention of returning at the end of the day to that particular field in the morning, make the last row you pick a long one. Forget the cotton—leave it on the bush— and when you get to the end of the row, keep going, and make sure you take the cotton sack with you. In the old days you picked cotton by hand, dragging the sack between your legs, stuffing it as you went. The farmer furnished the sack. You were paid, by the pound, right there in the field. As soon as the sack was full, you dragged it over to wherever the farmer had his scales set up, it was weighed, and your money was placed in your pocket right then and there. Empty, a cotton sack is about six feet long, and it is supposed to be just about the best thing in the world to sleep inside of.

I say *supposed* to be because although I have picked a lot of things, I have never picked cotton. I never *had* to. Over the years I was led to believe that this was a mark of achievement—never having had to pick cotton—since in the American West that occupation was just about the lowest rung on the job ladder. Compared to cotton, picking hops, pears, apples, and cherries practically made you an aristocrat.

Now I realize that I missed something. There was a world out there in those cotton patches in western America that was unique. Now that cotton is no longer picked by hand (all cotton is now picked by machine), the stories are beginning to come out. In addition to a lot of excruciatingly hard work, a whole life existed among the cotton pickers. People were born in those cotton patches and people died in them, sometimes violently. And some fell in love—"I met my wife in a cotton patch," one man told me. Everything in the world at large was to be found, out there in that cotton, and sometimes under it. However, I missed it, and when I go back among my fruit tramp friends and the subject of picking cotton comes up, I have to confess I am not an authority on the matter.

"What? You never picked no cotton?" The question is always put to me incredulously.

"No." I have to shake my head. "I never picked cotton." Invariably someone will crane his head around somebody else to get a better look at me.

"No *shit?* You never picked any cotton?"

"No."

After a general shaking of heads, I am forgotten and the stories begin.

"Where did you pick cotton?"

"Where *didn't* I pick cotton!"

"Ever pick cotton in Tulare?"

"Hell, yes, I picked cotton in Tulare. Why Tulare?"

"I picked cotton in Tulare one time coming right out of jail. They turned me out early in the morning, no breakfast or nothing, and there was this farmer waiting down at the end of the block. That's probably why they turned me loose. He and the cops probably fixed it up between them. Anyway, the farmer said he needed cotton pickers, I was broke and hungry, so I climbed into the back of his pickup truck along with a number of others and we rode out to his cotton patch. It was the second picking and there wasn't much cotton *there,* but all I wanted to do was make enough money to buy some groceries and then I was going to be on my way. I started down the first row just a-snatching and a-grabbing, but the picking was so bad that it was after midmorning before my sack began to fill up. Then, just as I was about to weigh in, I heard somebody say, 'Hello, honey.' I'd been working away at that cotton so hard that I hadn't noticed her, but when I looked up there was this little gal sitting in the dirt at the end of my row with her legs spread wide, wide apart.

" 'Hello,' I said.

" 'Hello, yerself,' she said. 'How'd you like a little lovin'?' I'd been in jail nearly a month and I was pretty hard up, but I knew she wasn't giving it away for free, so I told her right out that I didn't have any money.

" 'Sure you do, honey,' she said. 'You've got money

right there between your legs.' She meant my sack full of cotton, of course. They only paid about a cent a pound in those days, but I must have had sixty, maybe seventy pounds in my sack, and that was something.

" 'It's a deal,' I said, and I laid her right there between the rows on top of my cotton sack, soft as a mattress. When we were done, she rolled me off, dropped her empty sack, and grabbed hold of my full one. I laid there and watched her drag my breakfast and my lunch off to the weigh station.

"Pretty soon I commenced to realize that if I was going to eat that day I was going to have to pick some more cotton, so I got up and went back to work. Even though I worked all through the noon hour it wasn't until midafternoon that I had my sack close to full again. God, I was hungry. My stomach was growling and the only thing I'd had to chew on all day was a couple of wild turnip roots. Finally, my sack was almost full. I was getting on toward the end of a row and about to call it a day when sure enough I hear someone say, 'Hello, honey.' There she was, a different gal this time, sitting there at the end of the row with her legs apart.

" 'Nope, not this time,' I said, hearing my stomach growl.

" 'Are you sure, honey?' she said, pulling back her skirt and rubbing her crotch.

" 'You're on!' I yelled, feeling my pecker get hard, and we went at it, bouncing up and down on top of the cotton sack.

"I was the last person out of that cotton patch. It was almost sundown when I came dragging ass in. The farmer was about to fold up his scales and go home.

" 'Where the hell have you been?' he said. 'I haven't seen you all day.'

" 'Here,' I said, giving him my cotton sack. 'Weigh it and give me my money.'

" 'Why, you son of a bitch!" he said. "There ain't thirty-five pounds of cotton here. What have you been doing all day?"

" 'Never mind,' I said. 'Just weigh my cotton and pay me my money.'

" 'Pay you? Why, I've got two skinny little ol' gals out there who've picked almost five hundred pounds apiece. Pay you? You lazy bastard, I ought to take you back to jail where you belong.'

" 'Mister," I said, 'weigh my cotton and give me my money. I haven't eaten all day. I need that thirty-five cents for a couple of cans of pork and beans.'

"He flipped me a quarter. Two bits. 'Get off my property,' he said. 'And don't come back tomorrow. I don't even want you tromping up and down my cotton patch.'

" 'That farmer didn't know it and I didn't tell him, but he had some cotton patch. There was pussy growing out of the end of almost every row. I learned something from it, however. A young gal with an active snatch can make more money in a cotton patch than a strong man with a hard-on. And it don't matter if he's hungry or not."

After hearing an account like this, no one would conclude, of course, that spending a month in jail only to be freed to work your ass off all day in total hunger is a lot of fun. But these stories always bring forth bursts of laughter all around. And they always have a point to make, a moral, I guess. In this case, I suppose, it is to illustrate how impossible it is sometimes for a young man to keep his pecker in his pants. But they are best appreciated if you have shared that world of work. I, and perhaps the reader, have never put in time in a cotton patch, and a picking machine has ensured that we never will. But there is still a lot of work out there in the working world. I am certain there always will be. Those doing that hard work do not see themselves as victims seeking pity. They are simply fleshing out their lives with something more than meager wages for a lot of sweat. And they never fail, I have found, to temper irony with laughter.

CHAPTER SEVEN

The Enchanted Hard Hat

The hard hat is an amazing protective device. As the posters point out, the hard hat will protect the wearer from a falling object, provided, of course, that the object is not too big or too heavy. The hard hat will also protect you when you bump your head. If you work in a mine, down in the hold of a ship, or in dozens of other places one might think of where one finds low overheads, there is always something waiting to collide with your skull, raise a bump, and water your eyes. A hard hat will also, if placed on the ledge behind the backseat of your car where everybody can see it, identify you as someone who works for a living, and a lot of guys like to do that.

In spite of all this, practically no one I know likes to wear a hard hat. It is bulky and awkward on your head, and when you bend over it is always falling off. If you take it off, you are likely to forget it and leave it somewhere, and then you have to buy another one. And you had better not be caught without one, because most industries insist that all blue-collar personnel wear hard hats in all phases of work. In fact, in my industry, I know of no other safety campaigns waged with as much energy as the ones designed to get everybody to wear the damn things. Sometimes these safety drives leave us all wondering about management's true intent. Once while parked waiting for a friend in front of a factory I witnessed a man being told to put on his hard hat; he was mowing the lawn out in front of company headquarters, and I suppose there must have been some danger of the sky falling. Carried this far, the hard hat has become an amulet, a company-sponsored rabbit's foot or lucky charm.

It seems to be the firm conviction of most people—but certainly not always of the person injured—that accidents are avoidable. We are constantly admonished by posters, lectures, and slogans to exercise care, take precautions, and look before we leap in all phases of work. As if we have to be told. Strange things happen when someone is hurt. Although the person lying there bleeding is rarely assigned public blame for his accident, invariably the feeling is expressed all along the chain of command that if we would all just work harder at "safety," accidents would never happen. We are all, through some undefined power, supposed to possess foreknowledge and not to have been standing precisely *there* when that cable snapped and put one of us in the hospital. Certainly we would all like to have that power, and not just to stay healthy. If I had known yesterday what I know today I could, after all, have won the lottery or brought in a winner at the track.

Curiously, the people most involved with promoting safety—the safety committee personnel putting up all those posters—never seem to understand that accidents are built into the industrial process and that profit and loss are the principal factors. If you speed up the assembly line from sixty-two cars an hour to one hundred, accidents are going to increase accordingly. Or, more subtly, in my industry if the walking boss tells a gang of longshoremen that the shipowners would like the vessel to sail at three in the afternoon and that if they can get the work done by that time they can go home early with a full day's pay, then I can state to you positively—in writing—that the cargo will be stowed away by two-thirty and, by God, nobody had better get in the way of the hook.

But even without a speed-up it is impossible to work very long around machinery without sooner or later becoming involved in an accident. With luck you may be only a witness, but the sobering fact is that when heavy weights are being pushed, pulled, or lifted, something eventually snaps, jams, or simply tears itself apart. In the resulting equipment failure, quite often someone gets hurt. There is no question that occasionally the accident is the fault of the man operating the equipment; a slight misjudgment or lack of attention is enough to break someone's leg or lay waste to him entirely.

However, far more work injuries occur lifting heavy weights without machinery. That is, with your back.

Back injuries range from slight sprains, where all you feel the next morning is a little soreness, to destroyed vertebrae. The latter injury can be a lot more serious than the more dramatic accident where a bone is showing through a tear in someone's pants leg and blood is beginning to make a puddle on the concrete. Legs can be put back together with a remarkable degree of success. Backs cannot. There is nothing like going to the hospital and visiting a friend encased in a body cast from his knees to his neck to make you think about that office job you could have had if you had learned to type.

The annoying thing about injuries, all injuries, is that they stay with you. Maybe you did not end up in a cast, but all those little hurts that you suffered when you were a kid or in your twenties—the cracked knuckle, the separated shoulder, the twisted knee—and that you had long forgotten and thought healed come back to haunt you when you approach middle age. Around forty-five or fifty, sometimes earlier, you discover you have been favoring your left arm recently when lifting over your head because it is painful to do otherwise; or you are putting most of your weight on your left leg when pushing against a heavy object because your right knee has a tendency to fold under pressure. Fortunately the human body is such that by a careful selection of alternative muscles you can usually emulate a whole working man. Sometimes you may even find your aches and pains a bit ridiculous; if a heavy packing case is your moving problem, you and your partner may find yourselves circling it, around and around, like dogs preparing to lie down, each of you looking for the most comfortable way to push, pull, or shove. Eventually you will find a way to accomplish the task, and some men, old-timers especially, seem to be able to ignore pain and go on working forever. But if you have suffered a severe back injury, forget it. Use the disability insurance to get yourself retrained as a fry cook. And then watch out for hot grease.

Attitudes toward job injuries have changed over the years. These days, with disability insurance and workers' compensation, the financial hardship associated with lost time is eased somewhat, although it can still be a personal disaster. If you have mortgage insurance, even the house payment gets paid. If you have supplemental income provisions, you might possibly end up netting more money

than you did working. I know of a few cases where this
has happened. In this situation the younger worker is
likely to ride out the injury for as long as he is able to stay
off the job, frequently not without a little self-pity. The
older worker has a tendency to fret and to return to work
as soon as possible, sometimes prematurely, before he is
completely well. Old-timers, by and large, regard on-the-
job injuries matter-of-factly, as part of their life as workingmen.

When I first came on the waterfront, my partner and I
used to like to work in one particular gang that was bossed
by an old-timer whose last name was Sams. Sams had
gone to sea when he was fourteen. He had sailed square-
riggers when the deck crew worked barefoot so as to
climb the rigging more nimbly. He was a kindly man and
ran his gang with a smooth and easy competence that was
both instructive and pleasurable to watch. He called everyone under the age of forty Jimmy, and his knowledge of
ships and ship gear was so profound that it never occurred
to anyone to resent any order he might give.

Once, while we were covering up the hatch at the end
of the day, a five-masted Scandinavian sailing ship with
cadets crawling all over it came gliding into the bay and
made for the pier next to us. All work in our longshore
gang ceased, and we watched in admiration as the deck
crew hauled lines, dropped canvas, and swung booms
around with swift competence and precision. We were
used to a lot of huffing and puffing when a ship came in,
but the square-rigger slid right up and gently kissed the
dock without making the slightest use of a waiting tug-
boat. It was a remarkable performance, and I guess I must
have said so out loud.

"Yeah, would you look at all the gear?" my partner

responded in disbelief. Each mast had five sets of sails, and each set had its own hoisting gear. Blocks with tackle were running in all directions, not to mention shroud lines, apron stays, and God knows what else. "How do you suppose they keep track of it all?" my partner added. "For instance, that little sail way up top there on that first mast. What do you suppose they call that little piece of canvas?"

"Fore skysail," a quiet voice said behind us. It was Sams, the gang boss, half a smile on his face, staring across the water and caught up in the event as much as we were. "Just below it is the fore royal. Then the fore topgallant," he said.

While my partner and I turned back to watch the rest of the spectacle unfold, Sams continued on, ". . . fore upper topsail, fore lower topsail . . ." As we watched, three crewmen finished their tasks aloft. Grabbing lines, they swung out and slid all the way down the rigging, landing lightly on the deck. ". . . mizzen topgallant staysail, lower studding sail . . ." Sams was hung up. He and the sailing crew finished just about the same time. As the cadets completed their work, they disappeared below. Finally, the deck of the square-rigger became deserted.

". . . crossjack and spanker," Sams finished up. It was one of those times when I felt that applause might be called for.

"What was it like, Sams?" my partner asked, grinning. "What was it like in the old days to sail a ship like that?"

"Well, Jimmy," Sams said, staring past us to the masts and spars, the smile fading from his face, "if you survived long enough to learn how to do it right, it was mostly hard work."

"Survived?"

"We used to lose a lot of men," Sams said briskly. "You

know, to falls and suchlike. And if you were standing in a bight and a line started to run, sometimes before you could leap clear it would have you. If it caught you right it would snap your ankle like a soda straw. Maybe cut off your foot if you were unlucky."

Luck, fate, destiny, or whatever, with men of Sam's generation, physical injury was nothing to brood about. At times they might even find it good for a laugh. On another job, while standing by waiting to board a ship to go to work, Sams, my partner, and I were idly watching the ship's crew rig the gangplank. The ship was low in the water, with the deck almost level with the pier, and the main gangplank up the side of the ship remained lashed in its cradle. In its place the crew was rigging a short ramp leading directly from the dock to the ship's deck.

As we watched, Sams shook his head. "On the old steam schooners we used to use that short gangplank all the time," he said. "Sometimes when the tide was out, we even walked *down* to get aboard ship."

"You may get a chance to do it again," I observed. "The tide doesn't bottom out until nine-thirty."

"How about that, gaffer?" my partner added. "Just like old times, huh?"

"That's right, Jimmy," Sams replied. "Just like old times. Except in the old days we had to lift that gangplank by hand, and it was heavy. Took four men to a side." The seamen were using a power winch.

"I remember one time," Sams continued, "we were having trouble finding the slot in the rail so that the ramp would lock in place. We would heave forward, and go past it. Then we'd heave back, and miss it again. We had this fella named Billy in the gang, and finally, since the rail was about even with the dock, Billy leaped aboard ship and grabbed the end of the gangplank with both hands. 'All right," Billy says, 'we're about an inch short. Everybody give a heave and I'll guide it in.' So we all give a heave, and just as the ramp clicks into place, I hear Billy swear. We all troop aboard, and there's Billy holding up a hand, all bloody, with one finger missing. He'd got his hand caught between the plank and the ship's rail, and it had cut one finger clean off."

"Jesus!" my partner said. "That's awful."

"Well, like I said," Sams said with a shrug, "them short gangplanks was heavy." My partner and I waited, but Sams did not go on. It did not seem to me that the story should end there.

"What did Billy do?" I asked, not sure I wanted to know.

"Do?" Sams asked, puzzled. "What do you mean?"

"What did he do?" my partner demanded. "Christ! The man just lost a finger. What did he *do*—go get it sewed back on?"

"Oh," Sams said, looking thoughtful. "No, he didn't do nothing much of anything, as I remember. He just stood there holding his hand up, saying, 'I'll be goddamned. I'll be goddamned,' and staring at his finger, which was lying there on the deck, twitching. Finally, the blood began gushing out pretty bad, so he wrapped his hand up in a bandanna and went off to the doctor. Too bad, too," Sams added. "Billy missed out on the best part of a lot of work."

"Well, ain't that awful," my partner declared to me. "Billy missed work! That's about the worst thing that could happen to a man, missing all that work . . . and over one lousy finger." As he spoke, my partner stormed around in a circle on the deck, his fists buried deep in his pockets. I discovered that my arms were folded across my chest and my hands protectively tucked away from harm.

"No," Sams said, shaking his head. "He didn't lose the whole job. He was back working by the end of the week. We let him drive winches. I'll never forget," he said, suddenly grinning broadly. "We had this guy in the gang who liked to joke around a lot. He was always playing tricks on everyone—Andy, I think his name was. Anyway, unbeknownst to us he retrieved Billy's finger from the deck, and for the rest of the day that finger showed up in the most unlikely places. You might reach into your pocket for a chew of tobacco and pull out Billy's finger. It even turned up once in someone's lunch pail. That went on all day until someone fed it to a seagull."

"Oh, shit!" my partner said.

It is always good to know where you are. It strengthens a man to find his place in the world, wherever it is. Sams's story enabled me to understand, not without mixed feelings, perhaps, that I was not and never would be an old-timer, no matter how many years I lived and worked. So far, I am still relatively whole. I have had all the usual injuries, but I have not lost any part of my body. In the event I ever do lose a finger, say, I'll have more of a comment to make than "I'll be goddamned." I will probably scream bloody murder, and take six months off work. I also do not want my finger played with and placed in someone's lunch pail. I do not think I would ever want to *see* that finger again, but I would want it treated reverently, buried somewhere, perhaps. I definitely know that I would not want it fed to a seagull.

Wars and auto wrecks take their toll of everybody pretty much equally, but industrial injuries are the fourth horseman of the working class. This is brought home most strikingly when one goes directly from a middle-class to a workingman's bar. The number of men with missing eyes and fingers and with limps and scars increases sharply. But these are only the surface signs, the tip of the iceberg, so to speak. A lot of coal miners die in cave-ins, but a hundred times as many die of black lung. And finally it is not what kills you but what you live with that hurts most. A number of occupations have nemeses peculiar to them, and working women are not left out. If with long-shoremen it is bad backs, with waitresses and sales clerks at Safeway and Macy's as they grow older it is fallen arches, swollen knees, and varicose veins. So even if it won't relieve that waitress of her pain, it will make it a lot more bearable if you don't forget her tip.

It is simply not true that all accidents are avoidable. There is no way men—and now women—can tunnel into the earth in search of coal and not have the ceiling occasionally fall on them. There is no way you can lift a load off a dock and swing it aboard ship and defy gravity for-ever. There is no way workers can process chemicals and minerals, the toxicity of which may not manifest itself for a generation (or even longer in the case of asbestos), with-out shortening their lives and in many instances terminat-ing their days in agony.

For the injured and disabled, today is unquestionably better than yesterday, but injustices still remain. Although black lung is now conclusively connected to the mining of coal, almost all those afflicted with this crippling condition are still denied disability payments or retirement. Today, Billy would get eight or ten thousand dollars in compensa-tion for that lost finger. But the waitress is still out of luck. So is the cop directing traffic at a busy intersection and the warehouseman working the loading dock, both of whom

have grown dim-witted over the years from carbon mon-
oxide poisoning because they have inhaled too much
exhaust smoke. Well, perhaps the policeman can transfer
to the homicide detail, but the warehouseman needs something more than one more poster admonishing him to
wear his hard hat. Unless it is some new model I have
never heard of, a foolproof hard hat, an enchanted hard
hat with an ironclad guarantee of health and safety.

Chapter Eight

Endangered Species?

A hundred and fifty years ago in the United States, farming was the occupation of the vast majority (actually, about 85 percent) of the American people. The family farm was the basic and universal unit except in the South, where plantation agriculture was fostered by a slave economy. Then as now, American farmers not only fed the nation well, but created surpluses for export to a hungry world. Today, in contrast to 85 percent, this task is performed by only slightly more than 3.5 percent of our population. Industrialization was the process through which this transformation took place. Over the years, farm boys leaving the homestead for the factory in the city helped in part to create the machines that more than replaced their labor back on the farm.

As the farm population decreased, the industrial, or blue-collar, workers increased, until at the close of World War II they peaked at close to 60 percent of the working population in America. Also growing along with them and continuing to increase into the present day was the sales, service, and white-collar / pink-collar segment of working America. This nonindustrial work-force passed blue-collar workers in number over three decades ago and continues to grow. Industrial workers now total only approximately a third of the American workforce, and every year their number drops steadily, leading one to wonder if their fate might not eventually duplicate that of their farm brethren. It is conceivable that sometime in the foreseeable future those making their living in mine, mill, and factory might total something less than 10 percent of our population.

The political significance of this possibility in a modern industrial state making full use of automation as it develops is as yet unknown. As for nonwestern or third world countries, industrialization should lead them to develop pretty much along our lines, and they may even profit from our mistakes. In a socialist state, such as the currently disintegrated Soviet Union, the ramifications may have been revolutionary, or counterrevolutionary if one is of the Stalinist persuasion. The flag of the USSR, a red star embellished with a hammer and sickle, symbolized the political union of the two largest economic groups in that state. But that was 1917. We have no hard data on agricultural workers in the former USSR, but their numbers over the years have been dropping, too, and informed guesses presently put them at about 18 percent. Technologically, the Soviet Union, except for intercontinental ballistic missiles, always lingered behind the United States, but as its factories modernized—automated—its blue-collar workforce unquestionably dropped, too. Since the meaning of History is not yet clear, we do not currently know how much of the upheaval in the USSR was influenced by a demographic shift of workers away from agriculture and industry. However, Marxist ideology was always rigid, based as it was on class numbers existing seventy-five years ago. Perhaps it was simply overtaken by that same History.

Arguments have been made that no matter how the workers have been shifted around and the color of their collars changed, they, as proletarians, remain unchanged. A look into a modern office with row upon row of computers attended to by what unquestionably are workers would seem to support this. After all, whether it is a lathe or a keyboard, you are still tending a machine. However, I have some doubts about this argument. I do not think that it is a lathe or a keyboard that determines your class status, but what goes through your head while you are working at them. After all, you cannot expect the machine to do everything for you.

As a worker, I have discovered a very simple test to determine the class to which a person feels he belongs. (At least it works in America. In America the classes mix to a degree unknown anywhere else in the world. In another country you may never get a chance to meet socially enough members of another class to even try this test out.) Anyway, in a mixed crowd, where in addition to a sprinkling of blue-collar workers you might find a fair number of administrators and minor executives (it doesn't hurt to throw in a couple of doctors and lawyers, too), casually remark that you know plumbers who make thirty dollars an hour. It will be a conversation-stopper, believe me. And it is a true statement. I do know plumbers, my eldest son among them, who do make that much, or more. And earn every bit of it!

After a silence, the first one in the group to speak will probably be a minor administrator, and probably the one occupying the lowest rung on the corporate ladder. However he states it, what he will say is that it is too much. If he is employed by a bank or a savings and loan association he will usually add that no wonder housing is so expensive today with labor costs like *that*. He will neglect to mention, of course, that interest rates, real estate commissions, etc. add three times as much to the cost of a house as do the wages of carpenters, plumbers, and electricians. Or that a 1 percent rise in the interest on the mortgage loan will, over the life of the contract, cost the buyer more than did putting in the house's entire foundation. Or, finally, that only someone making thirty dollars an hour building a house can afford to purchase one. Neither will any doctor present remark on the fact that he will make the plumber's hourly wage in two minutes or less by writing a prescription after someone has stuck out his tongue at him and said "Ahhh."

The working-class members present will have a different reaction. Usually they will keep their mouths shut, but if pressed for a reaction, their thinking goes something like this: "Hmmm—thirty bucks an hour? Why ain't I making that?" They know in their bones that they will not raise their own wages by trying to lower someone else's. Most blue-collar workers also get a warm feeling, believe it or not, when they hear of some other workingman who is doing okay.

Trade unions in America almost by definition have been a blue-collar phenomenon. Their rise coincided with the industrial revolution and the triumph of the machine. The falling-off in blue-collar numbers probably is the reason for their decline, perhaps even signifying their eventual demise. What is clear, nevertheless, is that trade unions filled a blue-collar need, however inadequately at times, that came into being with the industrial wage earner and grew along with him.

But nowhere have we seen a similar organization rising to meet the needs of the white-collar workers as their numbers increased. The small number of white-collar trade unions that exist, with a few exceptions, are weak and ineffectual. In plain language, the vast bulk of white-collar workers do not see trade unions as an instrument they care to use to better their wages and working conditions.

Among the reasons given for the white-collar rejection of unions is that a large percentage of lower-echelon white-collar workers are women. It is implied that there is something inherent in being female that blinds a woman and prohibits her from recognizing and acting in her own self-interest as a worker. She, as female, has occupied a role of subservience over the centuries that has destroyed her ability to resist the bosses' authority and act independently. Womanly wiles, we are urged to believe, feminine charm and sexual favors, are what she falls back on, and since such wiles are practiced individually, she is incapable of banding together with other women in a concerted effort for mutual gain.

These charges are ridiculous in the light of the activities of working-class women over the years. I have worked with countless women on many, many jobs in my time, and when it has come down to trade union action and support the women have always stood up as willingly as the men. Frequently more willingly.* As for trade union

* Women field workers in the United Farm Workers under the late Cesar Chavez are a good present-day example of what female trade union workers are capable of. In addition to working in the fields side by side with men, they place themselves in the forefront in strike situations. Frequently when violence is imminent you will see only women present on the picket line, the UFW theory being that the cops will crack men's skulls where they would not bludgeon women, or will be more reluctant to do so and will take it easy on them. This has not always held true, and some union women have taken terrible beatings over the years.

action in an emergency, I once knew a woman who had even served on a goon squad in a strike of the lettuce shed workers years ago. She carried a brick in her purse and battered the hell out of more than one scab she caught crossing the picket line. A favorite technique of hers was, in the company of a couple of backup men, to follow a scab into a saloon after work and dump him in there. "Hi, honey," she would say as she wedged herself in at the bar next to her target and laid her purse in front of her. Then, "Whomp!"

Another reason given for the failure of trade unions to catch on with white-collar workers is that unions are a working-class institution and white-collar workers see themselves as middle-class—they would demean themselves by joining one. Unquestionably there is some truth in this argument, but not enough to explain the huge mass of unorganized office workers toiling away out there in America earning only approximately 50 percent as much money as organized blue-collar workers. Even those white-collar workers who would feel demeaned by union affiliation have examples of other organizations in which they would feel comfortable and which serve most of the purposes of trade unions. It is not membership in an organization as such that is demeaning. Doctors who belong to the American Medical Association, for instance, do not appear to have greatly diminished their prestige.

What is clear is that what happened to blue-collar workers historically has not happened to white-collar workers. When the industrial revolution came along and European peasants and American farmers went into the factory and became industrial workers, profound changes took place in these individuals. Answering the factory whistle and tending a machine recast these men, and the lesser numbers of women who went with them, into a cohesive social group capable of uniting to respond to their environment together. Up to now, white-collar workers have had no similar experience of common feeling.

One would think that computer operators, banding together, could by withholding their labor bring an enterprise to its knees as fast as any group of lathe operators, thus bringing to themselves rising wages, better working conditions, and more fringe benefits. But it has yet to happen. It would appear that white-collar workers are vulnerable to even fewer threats than their blue-collar counterparts—a lathe can be moved to South Korea; a computer, whose product is continuously used data, is less easily moved. I have no explanation for the lack of common movement among our white-collar workforces. Neither have the union organizers from the AFL-CIO with whom I have talked. They just shake their heads. "What in the world is the matter with these goddam people?" I heard one say once after a failed organizational drive. I can only offer the opinion that it probably cannot be accomplished by an outside union organizer—that it will have to come from inside the workplace, and only after those wearing a white collar go through their "industrial revolution."

CHAPTER NINE

Leveling the Playing Field

How can someone, hour after hour, day after day, year in and year out, tighten approximately the same nut to the same bolt and not go mad? That most working people do not go mad is due in part to a phenomenon so common and so widespread that it is found the world over wherever people labor in industry.

Taking it easy on the job while someone else covers your work, or working on and off, as it is usually called in America, is an established part of work. It takes some kind of real mental case to do all the work he can all day long. No one expects it. Certainly not management. Managers might want it, but they do not expect it, and workers do not disappoint them.

Working on and off has its limits, however. The rules are infinitely varied, subtle, and flexible, and of course they are always changing. In spite of this, they are at any given moment usually very well defined. Management, up to a certain level, at least, is aware of the practice and in some industries employs entire cadres of people to curtail or put an end to it. Simultaneously, the workers are subtly doing all that is possible to keep it going and extend it wherever possible.

Every worker knows to a pretty fine degree how much work is expected of him. When he feels that the expectation is excessive, he tries to do something about it. This does not mean that all jobs end up getting the same input of work, of course. The men who lift the coffee sacks do more work than the man who sews up the occasionally ripped burlap bag. Nor does it mean that the same job gets the same amount of work in different places. For instance, longshoremen in Galveston, Texas, work harder than do longshoremen in San Francisco or New York, or so I have been told by men who have worked in these ports. Although my informants, all of whom are black, never say precisely why work is harder in Galveston, other than it is faster-paced, I suspect it is due to race. Down there the gangs are still segregated—one hatch white longshoremen, the next black—and they are placed in competition with each other to hold down their jobs. There may be compensations in Galveston, other than bragging, that I am unaware of, but no one I have talked to was eager to head on back down South. But wherever they are, most workers have a pretty good assessment of their own reality. And, of course, wages and the good things they will buy vary all over the world.

If management, through ingenuity or strength, sets up a situation, say on an assembly line, where a worker has another job pressing down on him just as soon as he finishes the one before, and he is having a hard time keeping up, the worker is not the only one in trouble. Very shortly there is going to be a power failure, or the machine is going to need readjusting, or the ominous, ever present monkey wrench is going to end up in the gears somewhere. If management repeatedly fires one worker because he cannot keep up and replaces him with another worker in the same job, that simply tells me that management is motivated by something other than production.

There are exceptions to this rule, extreme conditions. Historically, management has at times enjoyed situations where it had everything its own way. When the alternative is starvation you can make a person do anything you want him or her to do, as the Nazis demonstrated in their concentration camps. However, the desired end in the German enterprise was death and not production. If it is production management wants, then at the very least management has to let you earn enough to buy food enough to remain strong enough to work—so management can achieve production. This has a historical precedent, too. In nineteenth-century England the mill owners and mine owners managed to achieve this very delicate balance: the workers, men, women, and children working fourteen hours a day, were earning only enough to barely stay alive, and for only a very few years.

The factory managers do not have this balance now, at least in the western world, and they probably will never get it again. Not just because the British and other workers have a long memory, which they do, but because of the modern worker's understanding of the political nature of work itself. The bosses want, require, more from the worker than they give in return. The workers give work and the bosses give money. They are never quite equal. This discrepancy is called profit, and since the bosses cannot do without it, it is what gives workers their edge. A good worker in a key spot can, so long as he keeps up production, take all the coffee breaks he wants and the bosses will very likely look the other way. He could, if he wanted, cut down on the coffee breaks, apply himself, and increase production, and then ask for and get more money. But that is self-defeating, and he knows it. It also places him in competition with other workers, which is playing into the bosses' hands. What he would rather do is create some slack and enjoy the job more.

At present on the West Coast of America when a gang of longshoremen working breakdown cargo start a shift, they divide themselves into two equal groups and flip a coin. Depending to some extent upon the port and the work situation, one group goes into the far reaches of the hold of the ship and sits down. The other group turns to and starts loading cargo, usually working with a vengeance, since each one of them is doing the work of two men. An hour later, the groups change places. In other words, although I and my fellow longshoremen are there and get paid for eight hours, on occasion we work only four. (It actually amounts to five or six hours or even more most of the time, because it takes a full gang to rig gear, drop lashings, and so on to get things moving). If there is someone reading this with a swelling sense of moral outrage because we are sitting down on the job, I am sorry, but I have searched my mind in vain for a polite way of telling him to go to hell. Further, I would recommend he abandon his outrage and begin thinking about doing something similar for himself. Probably he already has, even if he won't admit it. For the guy who has not, however, here are a few pointers, because it is not all that easy.

To begin with, bosses are not dumb. If you think you are going to goof off all day long every day you work, you are out of your mind, unless you are the boss's son. Management is going to get more out of you than it gives in return. This is a fact of life, and one might as well accept it. If management does not get more—for instance, if it gets less—then why in the hell should it stick around? Your goal is to see that management does not get *too much* more.

Sometimes it is not easy. Sometimes you have to take a lot of heat. Management strives to set up a situation where work is done in series: a workman receives an article of manufacture, does something to it, and passes it on to another worker, who does something else to it and then passes it on to the next guy, and so on. The assembly line is a perfect example of this. Managers like this type of manufacture because it is more efficient—that is, it achieves more production. They also like it for another reason, even if they will not admit it: it makes it very difficult for the worker to do anything other than work.

If you find yourself in the middle of one of these series, whether you're operating a machine or merely doing something to the product as it passes by you, and you are having a hard time keeping up, you have only a few choices. You might go to the worker next up the line, where all the stuff is coming from, and ask him to take it easy on you. This would probably be your first impulse, especially if you have noticed that he is handling his job okay, with enough time left over to check the sports page briefly and carry on a conversation now and then with the guy working opposite him. But all he will tell you is that the stuff comes to him at that speed and he is only passing it on. He might give you a stare of contempt, but he probably won't call you stupid, because he would rather get along with you. He is right, too. In fact, the whole workload and pace may be started and maintained for hundreds of people by someone whom they never see who presses a button hidden somewhere about the plant.

If the person next to you is having a hard time keeping

up and the same goes for some others up and down the line, then you might get them all together and do something about it with a work stoppage. Or if you are organized into a trade union, all of you can get the shop steward to come down there, and he may do something about it. He might not, though, for various reasons. With or without the shop steward, you might take some action—wildcat strikes occur all the time—but for the sake of illustration, let us suppose that everyone else on the job is relatively happy and you are the only one that is feeling any pain. What can you do?

First, it must be understood that there is *no iron law of nature that says a machine must not stop.* If the only way you can get any relief is by breaking the machine, my advice is to make sure you do a good job of it and try to cover yourself as much as possible so that you do not get caught. Before breaking the machine, however, I recommend that you first try merely slowing it down. If you are having a hard time staying with it, your own limitations will help you here. Just relax and let the work pile up. You will get immediate results, since the man beyond you probably cannot do his job if you have not done yours, and so on down the line. If it's little red wagons you are working on, very shortly they will be coming out the other end minus a wheel, or whatever.

This also relieves you of the need to call the boss; he is already there, standing right behind you. Also his boss and probably several others. You will be aware that you are experiencing one of those periods in the day when you are not suffering from a lack of adequate supervision. Actually, this is what you want. In fact, you want all the bosses there you can muster, and the bigger the boss the better, because you want a boss present who is sufficiently high up to make a decision about changing the work. If all you get is the foreman, he will merely join in and help you with your job until you catch up. Not only does this defeat your purpose, but before he leaves the dumb bastard will probably even expect you to say thank you.

You want to attract all the bosses you can, and once you have them there you demonstrate with earnest industry that you are a hell of a good worker, that you sure are sorry about all this but, as any fool can plainly see, there is just too damn much for any one person to do, as good as you are at doing it.

At the end of this phase, it is now up to the boss. He can do one of three things: he can fire you, he can put another person in your job and transfer you somewhere else (which may be what you want even if it means less money), or he can get you some help, another person. You know which of the three you want, and if it is the last, you try to influence the boss's decision in that direction.

You have a choice of time. Midmorning is good—say about ten-thirty. The boss is aware that if he fires you now, the assembly line still has to get through the shift to the end of the day, and God knows what will happen. Midmorning is also good because it breaks up the day, brings on the lunch hour that much sooner. Maybe you would rather break up the afternoon because you find afternoons harder to get through, generally, than mornings, but that puts the action closer to the end of the shift and management has less to lose by firing you. You might not want to gamble with those odds.

What you want is another man to help you, and when you get him the two of you make damn sure you both are busy, at least until everybody goes away. Then, after the new hand has been broken in and knows how to do the job, you can tell him to cover you while you go take a leak. Then you can go over and stand for a while in the spot of sunshine that comes through the skylight, or talk to a friend, or even piss perhaps, before you go back and cover the new guy while he does the same thing.

Seamen, who have observed longshore work all over the world, tell me that working on and off is a universal waterfront practice. I have less knowledge of foreign factory work, but from what I have been told by those who have labored in European industries or witnessed work there, working on and off was usually present to some degree, with the practice most open and institutionalized where men, usually young, were doing the hardest jobs working together. Whatever else one can say, too many people work too hard for their meager living. But as for the work itself, within the group doing it it is always divided up fairly.

Curiously, management is not the only force aligned against the on-and-off system. With rare exceptions, trade union leaders are also opposed to it. This is not hard to account for once you remember that whatever their origins, they no longer make their living the same way as the men and women under their care. Also, the practice of working on and off cannot be a matter of negotiation in union contracts. Contracts address themselves to work, not leisure, and the multitude of subtle on-the-job perks stymie trade union negotiators at contract time; their imaginations in this area are limited to annual vacations. Furthermore, in order to divide the work fairly among themselves the workers have to organize, and once organized they might throw out their current labor leadership and get someone new. In those few instances where trade union officials have tried, either because of rank-and-file agitation or pure wisdom, to bring the contract closer to on-the-job reality, they have usually failed. The employers were adamant . . . NO!

Management knows where its interests lie. Some years ago on the West Coast, in negotiations on an industry-wide basis, the longshoremen's negotiating committee, bowing to company demands to do away with the on-and-off, tried to get the employers to accept two "coffee breaks" of fifteen minutes each, one in the morning and one in the afternoon. The employers flatly refused, and this question was at an impasse until it occurred to someone to reword the demand. It was immediately acceptable to the employers to give two fifteen-minute "relief" periods to the men, meaning this was the time you could go to the toilet.

This would seem to indicate an extremely close understanding of the workings of their industry on the part of managers, closer certainly than that of their trade union counterparts across the table from them. Except for recognition of man's need to answer a call from nature, they permitted nothing in the working agreement not directly connected to production. They knew, of course, that those fifteen-minute periods were going to be used for coffee breaks, naps, and whatever else the men wanted to do, and that the men would, as they had always done, go to the toilet at whatever time of the day they wanted, since nobody is going to stand there and wet his pants. What management wanted was to channel and confine the off time and reduce it, if possible, to only half an hour a day, and in this it was somewhat successful, since trade union negotiators also consider bargaining sessions as a trading contest and they gave up something for those fifteen-minute breaks, which the workers, in one form or another, already had.

What they agreed to in this instance was a reduction in the manning scale. Formerly where a longshore gang had eight men in the hold, in many ports they now had six. Since six can be divided by two just like eight, they could still try to work on and off, but it was a lot harder to do so, one obvious reason being that six men had to do the work formerly turned out by eight. Since machines had been introduced over the years, there were mitigating factors, but all things considered, the bosses won that one. After the contract was signed, the union joined with management in enforcing the contract—the "good faith" clause—and production fell not at all. Two jobs were eliminated from the world. Those two anonymous workers, wherever they are—I hope not on welfare, but a lot of people are because of these kinds of "deals"—suffered along with the other six.

Frederick W. Taylor, the efficiency expert who early in this century pioneered the time-and-motion studies that led to the assembly-line process in manufacturing, tried to reduce workers to robots, all in the name of greater production. His staff of experts, each armed with clipboard and stopwatch, studied individual workers at their appointed tasks with a view toward eliminating unnecessary movements. Even ditch-digging could be made more efficient, they bragged, as if discovering something new in the world. Place the shovel, sink it into the earth with the arch of your boot for a good bite, and heave out the dirt. Then place the shovel on the earth again, etc., etc. Don't lean on that shovel between times! That's an unnecessary movement! The Taylorites quickly discovered that they were being met with a great deal of opposition from some very tired workers, and that the best subjects for their work experiments were healthy young adult males who were mentally retarded. They accepted direction readily and evidenced less boredom from repetitious acts. Even they tended to goof off when the staff member wandered away somewhere to have a cigarette and shoot the breeze with a colleague. But when a staff member was present, they got some pretty healthy shoveling done, even if it took two men, one only watching. Any knowing worker's response to this situation would have been to put both men to work shoveling. On and off, of course.

Recently white-collar office workers have come under criticism for robbing their bosses of their full-time services. Too much time is being spent around the Mr. Coffee machine, and some people, would you believe it, have even been having personal conversations on company time. In fact, one office-systems expert recently said that he had yet to encounter a business workplace that was functioning at more than about 60 percent efficiency. Well, all I have to say to him is, Good luck, Jack, but I don't think you're going to find mentally retarded workers who can type very well, much less run a computer.

Working on and off is a very old custom. It is interesting to note that even the ancient galley slave rowed only half the time. I can imagine that imperious Roman commander, standing up there on the quarterdeck where the cool breezes blow. All he had to do was look over the side to know that only half the men were rowing. In his case, he may have regarded the men as less than human, mere beasts, but he usually let it pass as long as the vessel was moving along. When he did send down the men with the whips, he made sure they did not lay them on too heavy.

No employer is going to deliberately damage his own machinery.

Most people not directly engaged in daily work express disapproval when they hear of some particular group who are working on and off. A studied campaign with carefully chosen language—"featherbedding," "a full day's work for a full day's pay," "taking a free ride," "paid witnesses"—has been built up by the employers to discredit the practice, and their success is such that I very rarely discuss it except with other workers. My response is personal and I feel no need to defend it. If I am getting a free ride, how come I am so tired when I go home at the end of a shift?

Chapter Ten

Bosses

Ain't life gran. Six munts
ago I couldn't spel formin.
Now I are one.

—*Penciled note on the wall of a
factory washroom*

Actually, foremen and other bosses are neither
good nor bad. They just are. A boss may be
personally a decent fellow, or the world's foremost bastard. Also, he may have been hired (or
elevated) to his position to make use of either
of these characteristics. In those plants and factories where management has total control or
approach having it, the bosses tend to be or
approach being total bastards. In those work
situations where the workers are strongly organized and identify with each other, the bosses
tend toward being nice guys. It is not hard to
figure out why. In a situation where management can do what it wants, it hires bosses to
make the workers do what it wants them to do.
If the workers are strong and resist, management has to get along with them, and it hires
bosses who can get along with them. Or it permits the kindlier fraction of its bosses' character
to come to the fore in the bastards it already
has.

Frequently bosses and workers end up covering each other. For example, in that telephone factory in Illinois where everyone was quitting early, obviously the foremen knew all about it. There were bosses all over that floor, of course, and when late afternoon came and all the workers started cleaning up their workbenches, those bosses knew what to do. They made themselves scarce. They had forms and reports to fill out, and they took off for their own little area where they could work without being distracted, and without being confronted with idle workers, which might compel a response. If they did not have anything to do, then they invented something to do. Maybe they just went to the toilet—the bosses' toilet. Bosses usually have different toilets from the workers, and this is good because bosses need somewhere to hide and find some peace and quiet too. Anyway, the workers did their work in a hurry and quit early, and the bosses knew all about it. They went along with it for the simple reason that they did not have a choice—they were caught in the middle.

When a man is hired as a boss, it is made clear to him by management, by a superintendent usually, what his function is: he is to supervise production, make sure that the work gets done and that it gets done right. Along with these orders he is also told that there is room for improvement. I have yet to hear of a boss being hired who was not told just that. Maybe the boss he replaced was promoted to a position of greater responsibility, meaning that he was doing his old job at least okay. But the new man is invariably told there is room for improvement. "Things are getting sloppy around here. There's too many people hanging around, doing nothing and wasting time. Now, Al, I'm giving you a chance to see what you can do." Implicit in this speech is the threat that if improvements are not forth-coming Al will soon be back working at his old job again, getting dirty and earning less money, making the wife and kids suffer, disgracing himself, and probably ending up a jobless drunk sleeping in doorways. This is why so many bosses new to the job rush around raising hell with the workers under them. After a while they usually settle down.

Once again, the reason is production. Given an order to keep everyone busy at his work all day long, a boss, new or old, might just succeed in carrying it out, provided he is also given a big enough whip to do the job. However, if the resulting burst of activity on the part of the workers does not engender a rise in production, the boss has not done himself any good. And if production *falls,* he is in trouble.

"What's happening around here, Al? When I made you foreman six weeks ago I expected a little more from you in the way of results."

"Yes, sir. I hope you notice I've got everybody working now, sir. No more of that goofing off. I've got everybody on the job all day long."

"Yes, Al, but production has actually fallen. And now we're getting complaints from quality control. Too many units are coming out of your department showing sloppy workmanship. You'd better get to work on that, Al."

"Yessir." And that is all Al *can* say. If Al is going to work on *that,* however, he is going to have to come to terms with the workers, at least somewhat. The next thing you know, everybody is back to wrapping the work up early again. The superintendent will know all about it, of course, and with that knowledge the burden of the problem has now been transferred to him. His choice, finally, will probably be production. He may not give up without a struggle—he may even replace Al—but if the work situation remains the same, he will have to come to terms with the workers, too. Since the superintendent also has a boss over him, it may go all the way up to the factory manager, who probably initiated the crackdown for a "full day's work" in the first place. Finally, one day when the manager looks out the window and sees people slipping away early, knowing full well that they have arranged for someone else to punch their time cards, he will turn away with a shrug. Who's getting hurt? Production is okay, and the firm is making money. The only people suffering, possibly, are the stockholders, and they're probably all in Bermuda.

It does not work out this way every time, as we all know, and frequently the workers lose or receive a setback, usually because of circumstances beyond their control, such as automation, economic recession, or the factory pulling up stakes and moving away. Where the only change that takes place is in personnel—bosses—the workers can usually hold their own. However, it is a constant fight.

When they think about it, practically all workers dislike the idea of "bosses," people telling them what to do. On the other hand, management rarely has a problem finding candidates for promotion. "Getting ahead in the world" is the usual explanation given for why they take the job, by which they mean more money and the so-called prestige of being empowered to tell someone else what to do. This explanation is good enough for someone caught up in the getting-ahead bind, but even there it does not explain very much. Workers are not management trainees fresh out of college, and definitions of getting ahead in the world have a tendency to vary. Also, everyone cannot be a boss; there are not that many openings. From my own observations, I can state that for every worker hoping to get promoted to foreman, there are five others scheming to get themselves transferred from the job they are on to another job that is easier or more interesting. This is why seniority clauses are such burning issues to workers in all trade union contracts. It gives everyone hope for the future. Getting promoted to foreman is only one of a number of ways of escaping from a job that is dull, hard, and dirty. Whenever opportunity comes along, well, man, grab it!

There are exceptions. I have known a number of workers who flatly stated that they would not be a boss and then proved it by refusing the position when it was offered to them. These men are usually older, are usually good at what they do, and frequently have some very large interest or work outside of their job. They are happy enough with the money they are making and their job, and they do not want to upset the balance they have achieved in their lives. They are older men because it has taken them some years of maneuvering and seniority to get the job they at present have. They are good at the job because, first of all, that is the smartest way of keeping it and, secondly, the tasks they perform are interesting enough to present a challenge and keep them wanting to continue. The outside interest is made possible by the fact that the jobs they have are such that at the end of the day they aren't so drained of energy and emotion that they can't polish rocks, go bowling, chase women, or whatever. With a job like that, the average worker will think twice before accepting a promotion to foreman. Once again, the work helps create the motive. A man's desire to be a boss burns in pretty close proportion to the onerousness of the job at which he is working.

There happens to be another category, smaller still, of workers who will not be boss. Lefties—that is, people holding left-wing political convictions—may steadfastly remain workers on principle. Their fate is interesting. If their shop union is left-wing and they answer the call to take part in the organization, they usually disappear into their new occupation. That is, they lose their worker attitudes, since any post they occupy in the union above shop steward usually calls for full-time duty and turns them into trade union functionaries. Left-wing bureaucrats, whatever their individual virtues may be, have something in common with all other bureaucrats: no matter how hard they work at it, the reality of their job has nothing to do with the reality of the jobs of the workers they supposedly serve.

If the worker is left-wing and his union is not, he may keep his integrity and definition as a worker, but other ills befall him. He frequently ends up a pariah, always in opposition to both the union and the company. His fellow workers get tired of hearing him complain about everything and effectively isolate him from both power and influence on the job. Always political, he thinks in terms of disciplined group action and long-term goals, whereas the other workers, fighting the same war in their own little ways, prefer chipping away at the problem and avoiding confrontation with authority. If the leftie is an intellectual or, worse, merely educated, this leads to further isolation. His interests off the job coincide very little with those of the people with whom he works, and there is always some distance between them, founded upon the workers' suspicion of what they do not understand and their bottom view of their lot in life: if you're so smart, what are you working here for?

These left-wing workers have a tough time of it. Regarded as a thorn in the side by union and management alike, they have very little on-the-job protection; if management moves against them, the union may secretly enjoy it and raise only a minimal squawk. That they survive at all is due somewhat to prudence, of course, but also greatly to the men they work among. Over the years they seem to become in part the conscience of their fellow workers, the embodiment of what things might have been but failed to become, like Christianity.

I once observed a powerful trade union leader attempt to destroy a man such as I have described, to deprive him of his union membership and consequently his job. For four union meetings in a row, the rank and file sat, deadpan, and listened to their revered top leader charge the man with everything from having been a scab to being a labor spy. When finally placed on the spot and forced to stand up and be counted, the membership overwhelmingly supported the man against their international president. He was regarded as a nut and a crank by most of his fellow workers, but they nevertheless kept him on the job. After all, they worked with the guy, and it was *his job.*

Bosses are frequently protected by the men under them, too. The young graduate student with the clipboard in the telephone equipment factory discovered for himself how the workers were fulfilling their work quota. Nobody told him. Not even the bosses. It is reasonably safe to say that there was a tacit understanding on the part of everyone in the plant to withhold the facts, the true dynamic of the work situation, from the study personnel. No one there— that is, no one whose life was connected to the plant, bosses and workers alike—wanted to upset the stability and balance of their workday. In all probability, no word was ever passed, no discussion ever took place, between the workers and their foremen regarding the study personnel and the research being done on them and their occupations. But it was understood by all that it was *not* in their interest to be cooperative.

Unquestionably the young man's discovery of early quits led to a major shake-up. Information once made public is hard to ignore. Quitting early was only a part of custom. Dragging out your work so that it lasted a full eight hours, instead of doing it intensively for six and a half, was so-called law. The "Supreme Court" in this instance was hardly impartial, since it was in fact the higher echelons of management. Their law, even though heretofore they may have been ignoring it, dictated to them that it now had to be enforced, and no doubt there were repercussions all the way down the line. The outraged cry of "a full day's work for a full day's pay" was heard in every quarter, one can be sure. The worker's response—"If I'm quick enough to do my eight hours work in less, what the hell difference is it to you?"—remained mute. The workers simply addressed themselves to the task of reestablishing a fair balance all over again, something they and previous generations had had to do countless times before. It does seem to me, however, that each time this gets harder to do. Each time this happens, management comes out better armed. In this instance, it was equipped with the study notes and reports. In short, all those clipboards.

On the waterfront on the West Coast, the promotional steps are from longshoreman to gang boss to walking boss. All promotions take place from within longshore ranks. However, it stops there. Although there are numerous superintendents of various grades above walking boss,

and although there is nothing prohibiting it, no longshoreman to my knowledge has ever become a superintendent.
Admittedly, very few would want it; as a longshoreman,
gang boss, or walking boss, a worker is the member of a
powerful trade union that guarantees him a job until death,
whereas a superintendent can be fired tomorrow. There
is another, equally important reason: if a longshoreman
became a superintendent he almost certainly would take a
cut in pay. Supes are hired from all over, many of them
only recently out of college, and the stevedore companies
start them out cheap. I have actually worked at installa-
tions where the lowest-paid guy on the pier was the man
who was in charge of everything, or thought he was.

What this means in practical terms is that a very rigid
class structure is built into the waterfront. Walking bosses,
gang bosses, and longshoremen talk alike and dress alike,
essentially in work clothes. Superintendents frequently
dress in suits and sport jackets and wear shiny white hard
hats with their names printed on them. If this dress code
fosters an us-versus-them attitude, it does not necessarily
mean that the walking boss is on your side. It is always the
walking boss who fires you, sends you back to the hiring
hall where you get in line for another job. On the other
hand, the walking boss, having come up through the
ranks, recognizes and accepts waterfront customs and
work rules to a large degree. The stevedore companies try
to hire strong walkers with a lot of longshore years behind
them and then pretty much turn the ship over to them to
be loaded the best way they know how. This creates a
superintendent who is there largely for decoration. If the
line of authority becomes confused, it tends to be in the
usually young superintendent's head.

My partner and I once drew a job in a gang loading

hundred-pound sacks of rice. We were going up with them in pretty high tiers. At the end of an intensive hour's work, wet with sweat and panting, we fell out on some sacks to recover while the two other longshoremen in the team took over. A short while later the walking boss, followed by a young superintendent, came down the ladder. The walking boss immediately began checking the sacks of rice to see how much space he had left in the hatch. The superintendent saw us and headed straight for my partner and me.

"Why aren't you working?" the superintendent demanded, standing before us with his hands on his hips. My partner and I, still breathing hard, chose not to reply. He posed the question again. We continued to ignore him. All work in the hatch gradually wound down and stopped. The walking boss came over, nodded to my partner and me, and turned to the superintendent.

"What's wrong?" he asked.

"Either these men get up and go to work," the supe said, "or they're fired." My partner and I pulled ourselves to our feet, gathered up our jackets, and prepared to leave.

"Hold it," the walking boss said firmly to us. "Come here," he said to the supe, taking him away so they could talk in private. They stopped a short distance away by the ladder, the walking boss speaking quietly. We could not hear everything that was said, but we picked up enough to get the general drift of it.

". . . and we have to get this ship out . . ." from the walking boss.

". . . I have my orders," louder, from the supe. ". . . no more on and off . . . we had a meeting this morning . . ."

". . . twenty-five tons an hour from this gang . . ." from the walking boss. ". . . fire these two, and the rest of the gang will walk off, too. We'll need night gangs to finish the ship. . . ."

It was a classic longshore situation. The argument went on until the walking boss became enraged.

"Goddammit, get up that ladder and leave this gang alone," he said vehemently, giving the supe a boost up about three rungs. The supe was so startled that he continued climbing. Then the walker turned to us.

"All right, goddammit," he shouted. "I want this ship loaded out, and I don't want anymore horseshit from this gang. If we're not done by six o'clock, I'm going to fire everybody!"

"Yes, dear," I heard someone say from across the hatch as the walker climbed the ladder.

With this lack of control over your work, who the hell wants to be a superintendent?

The worst labor-versus-management situation I ever encountered was in an electrical wire insulating factory in which I once worked. The trade union was left-wing and management was rigidly antilabor. With or without the union, relations between the two entities, workers and bosses, had become so confrontational that most communications took place in writing.

We rarely saw bosses down on the factory floor. At the beginning of the shift, the three-man team of which I was a member would find our instructions taped to the machine we operated—such-and-such wire was to be processed using such-and-such insulating material. In a way, it was nice not having bosses around, but the machinery was so old and worn out that it was difficult to get anything done about even the routine repairs and servicing. The entire shift was spent by one or the other of us shaking the hamper to get the cold insulation pellets dropping correctly into the melting pot, checking the wire speed, which had a tendency to wander, and making sure insulation did not build up in gobs and turn out lengths of telephone wire looking like long black string beans.

Our written instructions at the beginning of the shift always required us to turn out 300,000 feet of insulated wire. Even without breakdowns we rarely exceeded sixty thousand feet. If run at capacity for a full eight hours the machine was still only capable of processing eighty thousand feet. After I had been there a couple of weeks, I asked my team leader, Ted, to explain this.

"That's just the shit that comes down from the front office," Ted said, dismissing the note from management. "We just do the best we can."

Ted was a very good employee, and he genuinely tried to get the best out of his machine. Ted did not dislike the company, even when the bosses did spiteful little things like requiring the workers to leave their lockers unpadlocked so they could be randomly searched (for stolen telephone wire?). To Ted, that was just the way companies were. Among the other employees, however, a state of pure hatred existed for the company and the bosses. When management tore off all the doors to the stalls in the men's toilets, someone went out and tore a door off a new Buick belonging to one of the bosses.

It was an oppressive place in which to work, and I was glad when cantaloupe season rolled around again and I could quit. When I returned in the fall, the plant was closed down. I looked up Ted. We had coffee.

Shortly after I left, our machine had broken down completely and had been retired from service. Several other machines about the factory floor had already met a similar fate. The company policy was not to replace them. It was a national corporation with plants all over the United States and with plenty of slack in production that could be made up somewhere else. What started out as an exchange of petty moves had ended up a fight to the finish. The company probably thinks it won. Actually, everybody lost.

CHAPTER ELEVEN

My Company, My Union, My Gawd!

As many people have observed, facts do not exist in a vacuum. If a so-called impartial group, say a department within a university, did an objective study of workers and work within a certain factory and then refused to make its research data available to the people who funded it, namely management, because of the uses the study might be put to, then management would simply go out and hire its own research staff. In most instances they would be the same people. Facts in themselves may be harmless, but not the uses to which they are put. Management has the power to make effective use of them, and it naturally ignores those facts which are not to its advantage.

Trade unions have now developed sophisticated research departments and put themselves into this arena, too, but with mixed results for the workers. In the past the United Auto Workers Union has demanded of General Motors, Ford, and Chrysler that they "open their books," with the end in mind of proving that their profits are such that they can readily afford a pay raise. Since workers are always happy to get more money, they make out all right in that direction, but they lose in another.

By opening the auto industry's books, trade union leaders open themselves to accepting the auto industry's view of the world. The gospel according to GM, Ford, and Chrysler, and all other industrialists, for that matter, has its own scripture, and all interpretations other than their own are heresy. The first commandment is that all salvation, for both parties, lies in increased production, since not only profits come out of production but also wages. Right? Trade union leaders, even those who feel uneasy with this line of reasoning, seem unable to come up with an argument to oppose it, or at least any counterdoctrine that has so far met with success. They may state loudly that they will not stand still for a speedup or an increase in the workload, but speedups and workload increases have always come to pass. In addition, union leaders have difficulty opposing automation. When technological change is completed, they tell themselves, they will discharge the duties of their office by jumping in enthusiastically for a share of the spoils for "their men." But what they get is not what "their men" always want. More accurately, the workers also get a lot of what they *don't* want. This only becomes apparent when the union representative takes the new contract, usually gleefully, back to the shop.

"Hey, Joe," he says. "We got you and Dave four bits more an hour."

"Yeah? Hey, that's great."

"And another week's vacation . . . after twenty years."

"I haven't been here that long."

"Yeah? Well, it'll make a difference later on. Now, we've agreed to let the company make a few changes around here. You and Dave won't be working together anymore. They're getting in some new equipment that combines several operations in one. Your machine will even have an automatic feeder. And you and Dave will be operating your own separate machines."

"Yeah? What's going to happen to old Pete over there? He's been our feeder a long time."

"That's the beautiful part of it, Joe. Pete's going out. It was a tough fight, but we got early retirement after thirty-five years in the industry. How about that?"

"Wait a minute. What about me? Are you telling me that I'm going to have to operate this dumb-ass machine all by myself all day long? Hey, wait a minute . . . hey, come back here!"

Ungrateful bastard, the union representative thinks to himself as he hurries away. And here I thought everybody would be delighted.

The curious thing about the "logic" of not just General Motors but the entire industrial production process is that no one questions whether or not it *is* logical, except the workers in their own unorganized, human ways. No one, to my knowledge, has even attempted to define "logic" in human terms. Is it logical that technological advance—that is, more efficient production—should always take place? Well, perhaps, but maybe not, depending upon its effect on people. Even if you want to reduce it to an equation and say, yes, more people benefit than are injured by a particular production innovation, does it therefore follow that when technology advances it has permission to do so at any human cost, however small, and that this cost must always be borne by those people most closely connected to the production process, the workers?

Should technological advance be permitted if it results in human cost to anyone anywhere? This is the question, and it is difficult to answer with a categorical *no*. *No* tends to stop the world, technologically, right where it is at this moment. Or at least slow it down. But if the answer is *yes,* those who bear the cost have the right to ask *why*. And further, if technological progress requires a human cost, is this truly progress? Trade union negotiators insist that this question comes up all the time in bargaining sessions when they negotiate with management. This merely emphasizes their failure, since nowhere is this issue addressed in the contracts under which everyone works.

What has become clear, at least in America, is that trade unions and their leadership have no program or ideology of their own. They only respond to the demands of industry and its management. After wage increases and fringe benefits, trade unions have exhausted their claims on the world we live in. Up to now we have waited in vain for unions to demand that some of the technological effort, now used exclusively to develop the machines, be used to benefit the workers who tend the machines.

Retiring earlier is great. So is another week off sometime during the summer. And more money—we all know what to do with *that*. But what about all those days of our years between the ages roughly of twenty and sixty-five, the longest and most significant period of our lives? It is precisely right here that the workers of the world meet the world's needs and create its wealth, and with each succeeding technological advance, these days become more of a blank in the whole of a worker's life. Shorter hours notwithstanding, the workday is the dominant fact of a worker's existence, and more and more he sees it not as a part of the life he is living, but rather as a large hole in the time he spends on earth, the price he pays for the bits and pieces of life he has left.

It is rightly said that machines have taken much of the sweat out of work. For instance, a man with a forklift can now load a truck while he sits on his butt, and perhaps get pleasure from it. But jobs like these essentially are backwaters to the mainstream of production. In those industries where technology has gone farthest and production is measured in hundreds of thousands of units—for instance, the auto industry—work, for the people doing it, is increasingly isolating and devoid of human interaction. As machines replace workers, those workers remaining are pushed faster and faster and are spread thinner and thinner, until now, in many places, they are hardly within shouting distance of one another.

If retirement is what you are mainly working toward, then you are living a mistake, serving out a jail term, so to speak, waiting for release. The work you are now putting in is dead time. Vacation in the summer is not even a parole, because you have to come back. All that money you are making? You could buy a new car. Someone has to, I suppose, since they keep coming off the assembly line.

Regarding work and leisure, people who call themselves humanist philosophers concern themselves, like trade union leaders, with a more equitable balance, that is, more leisure and less work for the worker through a greater share of the "abundance" created by the machine. But none of these humanist philosophers are tending a machine. Certain forms of escapist entertainment aside, leisure in itself is worthless without direction or content, and creative work can be more rewarding and fulfilling than many kinds of leisure. What is needed, it would seem to follow, is to rethink and readjust work to this end. Which is what all workers attempt to do daily on the job.

What is assuming tragic proportions is the frustration and defeat workers are suffering when they attempt to restore these qualities to their workday. Whatever the content of the contract presented to them for acceptance, it will be the joint product of management and the union and will contain nothing meaningful toward this end. Very likely, through management's assigned prerogatives, these human necessities will be reduced even further. You can vote the contract down, but the same people will be back in there negotiating again. The obstacles workers face are formidable: management and labor. The alternative is a huge body of unemployed living in semipoverty waiting for you to join them if you say no to the process and quit.

Every now and then one runs into someone who has a job he or she genuinely enjoys—"Yeah, I like my job. Hell, it's a lot of fun." I am somewhat startled but always pleased when I hear this. It proves it can happen and that all work is not agony. But try introducing fun into a union contract and see what happens. I never tried for fun, but I once tried to introduce comfort.

After about fifteen years on the waterfront I began to run for union office and eventually got myself elected vice president of the Bay Area longshoremen. Longshore job disputes on the West Coast are settled through a joint Port Labor Relation Committee composed of representatives from both longshoremen and the shipowners. If some longshoreman commits a gross indiscretion on the job, he ends up before the LRC. The penalties can range from time off work to being separated from the waterfront completely. If a stevedore company screws somebody out of overtime, we try to get it back. Sometimes we succeed. My fifteen years of seniority also permitted me to take jobs out of the hold and on the dock part of the time, driving a forklift truck. The waterfront still had a number of very old lifts with solid steel tractor seats, which everyone hated. The seats were not only hard, but on a frosty morning they could be very cold. When our weekly LRC meeting was winding down once, I decided to see if I could do something for myself and my fellow forklift drivers.

"Can we get something done about these tractor seats on some of the old forklifts?" I asked, introducing the subject.

"Like what?" the employer spokesman, sitting opposite us, asked. There were four representatives from each side.

"Like getting them replaced," I said.

"What for?"

"For comfort," I said.

When the laughter died down, I tried another approach, but it was no use. Even my fellow longshore colleagues thought it was funny, which was a breach of etiquette; if you cannot support your brother on the committee, you are supposed to at least hang dead, betray no emotion. I once had to keep a straight face while our business agent defended a longshoreman accused of attempting to steal a ship's clock from the galley of the vessel he was working. When apprehended by the first mate, he was found standing in the sink with a screwdriver in one hand, attempting to remove the clock from the galley wall. He was pleading innocent. What about that screwdriver? Oh, that had nothing to do with the clock. He hated bugs. He was using the screwdriver to stab cockroaches. If I could keep a straight face through a defense like that, one would think that I had a right to reciprocal treatment from my brother longshoremen, but I failed to get my request seriously considered. The lift drivers heard about my effort, thanked me, and continued to handle the problem as always, searching about for an old burlap sack to put between their butts and the steel seats.

If you think comfort is not scant in the work scene, the next time you go into a big department store, look around you. That comfortable chair conveniently provided for you to sit in while your wife tries on a dress is for you and not for the sales clerks. They are prohibited from sitting in those chairs and they are deliberately not given any of their own at their work stations. No matter how long they have been on their feet or how tired they are, they cannot sit down. It is a company policy. And while they are being bright, smiling, and helpful they had better not get caught leaning on the display case while they "make the sale."

Automobile production has always been one of the most automated industries in the country. And it's also one of the industries most plagued with absenteeism. In some plants half the labor force fails to show up on Friday; damn near all of the other half take off Monday. Modern workers are just no damn good, one usually hears as an explanation. (However, these are the same workers who made America great, so what happened?) Don't they appreciate all those gains labor has made over the last seventy-five years? The eight-hour day? Overtime after eight hours? Fringe benefits?

To which one might reply: What fringe benefits? Over half of the new jobs created in America today are part-time; they offer no vacations, medical care, or retirement vesting. As for the eight-hour day, many industries are trying to convert to a ten-hour day, four-day week. After four ten-hour sessions on the assembly line, those workers are going to *need* a three-day weekend. However, I do not even have to ask them to know that those workers currently taking off Fridays or Mondays are all for it. They have already done their arithmetic and have come to the conclusion that if they are currently able to squeeze by on thirty-two hours of work a week they sure as hell can tighten their belts a little more and make a living working thirty; they won't be there Tuesday, either.

Given no other alternative to an odious job, I am all for shortening the work week, reducing the hole in their lives that work represents to so many people. The biblical condemnation of man to work that is hard, cruel, debasing drudgery has certainly proved binding over the ages. However, of all the work I have done, of all the jobs I have held down in my life, no matter how hard they were, how hateful, boring, even underpaid, I remember none that did not have some rewarding moments. For me, those moments alone soften that biblical fate.

The argument that it is not work itself but man's estrangement from the product of his labor that makes factory life so hateful today is only half true. The worker may be alienated from the product of his labor, but he is also denied—alienated from—the social interaction of working with other workers. For almost 150 years, Marxist thought addressed itself to the first part of the problem while ignoring the second part. It used to be argued that the socialist states, as yet only imperfectly developed, would one day remove all that is hateful from work and provide the worker with what he was missing. We could dismiss them by saying they had their chance, but what is more to the point is that, then and now, *factory work is remarkably similar wherever in the world you choose to observe it.* Under whatever ideology, capitalist, communist, whatever, industrial work is much the same. And factory workers do what they can to make it more bearable, all over the world.

It is not surprising that absenteeism has recently become management's biggest problem in labor relations. Management is too clever; it has brought the problem on itself. Men who work on modern assembly lines tell me that it is almost impossible to do anything other than your job, and do it the bosses' way. For approximately every ten workers there is an extra man standing by. But he works, too. He relieves each of the ten men in turn both in the morning and in the afternoon, and in between he fills in wherever he is needed, and the need for him is constant because of the speed of the assembly line. You might say that management has made a sacrifice, using eleven men for only ten jobs, but it recovered that loss by speeding up the assembly line by 10 percent. Pretty crafty of the M.B.A. who figured that out. That's why Joe wasn't there Friday. And that's why Jack, when he left for the weekend, said, "See you Tuesday."

CHAPTER TWELVE

Three Decades on the Frisco Waterfront

Times change. We all know and accept that fact. On occasion we even applaud it, because no one wants to live in a static world. Work changes too. Work, being central to civilized man's existence, provides for change, makes it possible. But, on the evidence, until very recently work over the centuries seems to have changed more slowly than any other of man's activities. There is on exhibit somewhere an ancient vase painting of an Egyptian sailing vessel taking on cargo. A gang of longshoremen are marching across a plank stretched from shore to the deck of the ship, carrying sacks on their shoulders. Well within this century bananas were still loaded that way in Central America and discharged that way in New Orleans and San Francisco. One hundred and fifty years ago in England, longshoremen scampered around inside huge cages, like hamsters, to provide mechanical power to raise cargo from the holds of ships. Now we have electric cranes and winches, and one man can lift thirty tons or more by depressing a lever. Men who resist change are thought foolish for it. The worker who views it with suspicion, however, does not always lack good reasons.

For over thirty years my work has been that of a long-shoreman in the Port of San Francisco. More accurately, I work on the waterfronts of the San Francisco Bay Area, which includes the Port of Oakland and a half-dozen smaller cities where ships tie up, including Crockett, thirty miles up the river, where the sugar comes in from Hawaii.

Fifteen years ago my job, like that of longshoremen all over the world, consisted mostly of loading or discharging sacks and crates of cargo in the holds of ships.

Our day began by rigging gear. After we had got the booms placed correctly, we would open the hatch, uncovering the main deck, the shelter deck, and perhaps the upper and lower 'tween decks if the ship had them. Once we were in the lower hold—if the ship was empty we started loading at the bottom, of course—the first thing the winch driver brought in was a low, sturdy four-wheel cart. After that came the cargo, usually on pallet boards. Landing the loaded pallet board squarely on the four-wheeler, we would push the canned goods, sacks of rice, bales of cotton, or whatever it was we were working back under the coaming to the farthest recess of the hold. Then we would start stowing cargo. Usually we would begin against a bulkhead and bring the cargo out, tier by tier, to the open square of the hatch.

Then, as now, before a longshoreman boarded a ship and went to work a number of other matters called for his attention. The first of them was getting the job. Although we do not start work until eight, we get our jobs in the hiring hall earlier, at six-thirty. There is also a night shift, which is dispatched at five in the evening for a seven-

o'clock start. Work is dispatched on a low-man-out system, meaning that the man who has worked least gets first
chance at a job. If you have worked more than anyone else
and there are not enough jobs to go around, you will not
work that day. Those who *do* go to work that day will
gain eight or ten work hours on you. If they pass you in
total hours worked, you will get a chance at a job before
them next morning. Even-steven.

A longshoreman gets his job from a dispatcher, who is
another longshoreman elected to that position. A dispatcher does not work on the waterfront; he passes out
jobs to other longshoremen who do. Once a year, everyone votes for him, or for someone else. Any longshoreman who chooses to do so may run for dispatcher. The
top half-dozen vote getters win the posts.

Starting with the men with the lowest hours in the port,
the dispatchers call out work numbers, and the men go up
to the window and get their jobs until all the work is filled.
If you have low hours and are among the first called, you
have a greater choice of ships and piers from which to
choose your job for that day. If, during the dispatch, a
dispatcher holds back or conceals good jobs and then gives
you one of them when your face appears at his window,
you have profited from his action because you are on his
friendly list. However, all of the men who get bad jobs
will probably vote for someone else at the end of the year
and your friendly dispatcher will find himself back on the
other side of the window working for a living once again.
Then when your face appears at the dispatch window,
looking friendly, the new dispatcher may wonder what
the hell you are smiling about, because he is handing you
a ticket for the day that says you are going to be lashing
vans with eighty-five-pound turnbuckles, one of the worst

jobs on the waterfront. Honest elections make for honest officeholders.

But say, for instance, that you are about halfway down the list of longshoremen seeking work that morning and there are still plenty of jobs left when you get to the window. The job tickets are in two piles. The longshoremen who live in Oakland usually like to work in Oakland, but you live in Frisco. Sometimes, when the jobs in one place run out, the Oakland men are compelled to work in San Francisco, and vice versa.

Nowadays the work is very much the same, wherever it is, but a few years ago the ships you worked—and the piers—made a difference. It became a guessing game, and sometimes a lottery, to pick a good job.

"What have you got on this side of the Bay?" you would ask the dispatcher.

"Pier Thirty-two."

"What else?"

"Piers Twenty-nine and Eighty."

"Gimme two at Pier Twenty-nine. Bailey's gang."

Every longshoreman has a work number. You would give your and your partner's numbers to the dispatcher and he would write them down on a job ticket, stamp the time of dispatch on the slip of paper, and pass it through to you. Then you would telephone your partner to tell him where he would be working that day.

Some things never change. When you wake them up, partners respond as if you were their worst enemy. Since you take turns going to the hiring hall, you might expect to be treated cordially, to hear the phone answered promptly in a cheerful voice, but it never happens. Usually the phone rings and rings until finally a sleepy voice says, "Huh?" (Sometimes, since the decision to work or not to work is the man's alone to make, the phone is not answered at all. My partner was usually reliable and would call me if he did not plan to turn to the following morning, but he was capable of shoving the phone under a pile of blankets before he went to bed, or placing it out on the back porch. Consequently, I knew that I had to let it ring a while if I wanted to get my man.)

"Yeah?"

"Pier Twenty-nine at eight o'clock. Bailey's gang. What took you so long to answer the phone? I was about to hang up and turn your job back in."

"You know better than to do that. Don't I always meet the hook?"

"Are you kidding?"

"At least I don't put the telephone in the refrigerator like you do."

"Pier Twenty-nine," you repeat, in case he was too sleepy to remember.

"What else did they have?"

"Pier Thirty-five and Eighty."

"Whadja get Twenty-nine for? Why didn't you get Pier Eighty?" Some partners, expecting the worst, are already hostile before they answer the telephone, perhaps with some justification. I once had a partner who *liked* to pick up the jobs and telephone me the news. I would get the message in one word, and usually it was a lie. "Bananas! Heh, heh, heh, heh," he would screech into my sleepy ear. Or "Coffee!" Or "Cotton, nails, and barbed wire!"

"It's too early for jokes," I would mutter. "Where are we really working?"

"Pier Thirty-two. Coffee. Heh, heh, heh, heh."

"Come on, now. Where are we really working?"

"Pier Thirty-two. Coffee. No shit. Bring your sack hook."

As partners go, he was a pretty good man to work with. On coffee we worked well together, anticipating each other's moves and making it as easy as possible to throw the sacks. Discharging coffee can be brutal, but he did his share of the work and more, setting up at least half of the sacks and lifting with me in an even, steady swing. He was a good man in a beef, too; if you got in an argument with a walking boss, he was right there with you and not hiding out somewhere behind cargo.

"Coffee, huh?" You always try not to shudder, but moving 154-pound sacks all day long . . . "Okay. Pier Thirty-two. I'll meet you there. Goodbye."

"Wait a minute! Hold on. Don't hang up."

I knew the bastard *so* well. When he did this, it was possible I had been given a reprieve. Possibly I was not going to work coffee after all. "What is it? Will you cut out the bullshit?"

"It ain't coffee. Would I get you a crummy job like that, old buddy?"

"Where are we working, then?" I would ask casually, trying to keep my temper. If I blew my top, it would just turn him on.

"Pier Forty-five. Raw hides and cotton. It's a long job. We'll be there a week." He was that kind of a son of a bitch.

But what if he was telling the truth? Cotton was okay. A bale of cotton weighs five hundred pounds, but we could handle it. Raw hides, however, were something else. Hides came from the hide house folded into a bundle with the hair in and the slimy side out, sort of loosely tied together with a string. Frequently they were crawling with maggots. To protect the hide from the maggots a scoop of manure from the steer was shoveled onto the center of the skin before it was folded and tied. On the voyage overseas the maggots ate the manure and not the hides. It saved the leather, but it did not make the hides much fun to pick up. You would grab a hide, give it a boost, and "pop"—you would have manure all over you. Or if the string broke at a certain point in your swing, you would drape shit all over your partner, always a conversation stopper. If he had gotten the job that morning he wouldn't say a word, but if you had been the one in the hiring hall and that happened, it might break up the partnership. Anyway, you had better not laugh.

On the other hand, I used to know a longshoreman, an old-timer, who did not mind hides. Not at all. I once saw him *volunteer* for the job. He was in front of me in line one morning, and when he got up to the window he actually *asked* the dispatcher for a hide job. I could not believe it, and I pestered the old man until he told me why. Hides weighed only fifty-five or sixty pounds—light cargo—but that was not the real reason. It turned out he did not own a car and he had to take public transportation to and from work. When you worked hides, even if it was for only an hour or two, you stank. People actually fled from you. When the old man went home at night, tired out, he never had any trouble getting a seat on the streetcar.

And now I had my partner telling me he had got us hides. "Okay. Hides. Eight o'clock at Pier Forty-five. I'll meet you there. Goodbye." But naturally I would not hang up the telephone.

"Wait! Wait a minute. Waaai . . ."

"Partner, where the hell are we working today?"

"Pier Thirty-five. We're loading ship's stores, an easy day. But that ain't the good news."

"It isn't?" I was helpless. Putty in his hands. He could play me like a piano.

"No sirree. The good news is that the ship isn't due in until nine o'clock, and then guess what? She's sailing at four, so we are going to get done early."

"Oh, God bless you."

"How's that for a job, huh? Your ol' partner did all right by you today, didn't he? Huh? Didn't he?"

"You sure did," I would have to admit, and then I would praise him, genuinely relieved that the earlier horror stories were untrue. "For once you showed some smarts around the dispatch window."

"Proud of me?"

"I'll tell the world. You are a partner to be proud of, a real gem, a real . . ." But there was always that *suspicion*. He could be treacherous. "Wait a minute, you son of a bitch. Are you telling me the truth?"

"It's the straight dope, so help me. Pier Thirty-five. Nine o'clock. See you there." Then, if I was lucky, he would hang up. When he hung up the phone I knew he had finally told the truth. On a rare and truly beautiful occasion such as a nine-o'clock start, this longshoreman would jump back into bed and sleep for another hour, thanking, before I slumbered off again, the patron saint of stevedores, and yes, my partner, too, and the Great Dispatcher in the Sky, from whom all blessings flow.

On other occasions, however, the news would make me cry. The phone would ring. Maybe I'd had a few drinks the night before and woke up feeling a bit thick. Or maybe I'd just been up late with my wife watching the late movie on TV. I would stagger around and find the phone, as welcome as death, pick up the heartless black instrument, and hear, "The copra dock. Pick and shovel. Eight o'clock." I would wait. "Okay," he would add, "I'll see you there. Goodbye."

"Hey, wait a minute," I would scream.

"What is it?"

"What did you say?"

"The copra dock. Eight o'clock."

"You're lying," I would accuse him hopefully.

"Not this time, old partner." Click.

Copra. The copra dock. Copra is dried coconut meat. It is rendered into oil that is made into a butter substitute. Discharging copra was all pick-and-shovel work. You picked while your partner shoveled. For spice and variety, you could always trade jobs. When you got this kind of a message on the telephone you might find yourself, sometimes twenty minutes later, sitting on the edge of the bed with a sock dangling from one hand, staring at your own poor reflection in the mirror on the closet door. Condemned, with no hope left, you would curse everyone in America who ate oleomargarine, and then get dressed.

If you are in the hiring hall, after dispatch you have a little time, perhaps as much as an hour, before you turn to and go to work. You gravitate to one of the coffee joints or restaurants near your pier. There, over steaming coffee, you can read the morning paper, doze, or exchange lies about your remarkable physical, mental, or sexual prowess with whoever will listen. As eight o'clock approaches, you all begin drifting toward the pier head.

Ships now are all pretty much the same, but a few years ago each one was different from the next. Even those vessels built as sister ships began getting altered from their first day of use. Flanges are ripped off here and welded on there. Ladders get moved from the center to the end of the hatch because of cargo requirements. After a few voyages, modifications of all sorts have taken place. But each ship also had a different *feel*. It is like two ten-year-old cars of the same make and model. Sitting in them is not even the same. One of them is missing a side-view mirror. The other has a door that sticks. Most likely they are painted different colors.

Crews have not changed, however, meaning they vary just about as much as do the maritime nations of the world. Many longshoremen used to have mixed feelings about working Philippine ships. The cargo was invariably good, meaning easy to work, and the jobs usually lasted several days, which we liked, but the decks and passageways were always jammed with old stoves and refrigerators, making it difficult to move around. Worse, wherever there were no stoves or refrigerators, from bow to fantail the space was taken up with barking, yapping tied-up dogs. Up until a few years ago, Filipino crews were paid very low wages. When we came aboard they would sell us fifths of scotch and cognac for five dollars that they had purchased in a free port somewhere for two dollars. Here in the States they would invest their profits from liquor in used kitchen appliances and double their money again when they got back home in the Philippines. The master of the vessel let them do it as compensation for their low pay. The dogs were there, of course, because they ate them.

Starting at eight o'clock in the morning on the first day of work on Philippine ships, we longshoremen would fill up the holds of the vessel and the crew would fill up the deck. All day long, small brown men would be carrying huge refrigerators up a narrow gangplank or dragging some dog, usually resisting and snarling, down the pier toward the ship. By sailing day the passageways would be so crammed with used appliances that you had to turn sideways to squeeze by, and every time you turned around you stepped in dog shit. We never knew whether to laugh or swear.

the official response by walking bosses and stevedore company executives to this deck cargo was to look the other way. It was ignored. Management personnel were always slightly embarrassed by this cargo, but the only time I ever saw the bosses take notice was once when some unknown longshoreman took his knife and cut all the leashes. The superintendent was pushed out of shape because twenty minutes was lost from work while the crew scampered about recapturing their livestock.

Although all the dog droppings probably constituted a safety violation—a hatch tender occasionally took a nasty fall when he stepped in some and his feet sailed out from under him—no longshoreman I ever heard of lodged a complaint in an attempt to curb the dogs. Most longshoremen have a live-and-let-live attitude and a working-class reluctance to intrude into the area where another man makes his living, and the Filipinos were left alone. Once, as a joke, I tried to bring up the subject with the union business agent, a sour, grim-seeming person until I got to know him better; he had the thankless job of making the stevedore companies live up to the contract. I encountered the man at the foot of the gangplank as my partner and I were leaving the ship. It just so happened that at that very moment one of the crew was approaching with two well-groomed poodles. Obviously the man had been foraging up on Nob Hill.

"Say, about these dogs?" I said to the business agent.

"Yes?" the business agent replied, eyeing me quizzically. "I guess you know what they do with those dogs, don't you, son? They eat them."

"Yes, I've heard that," I said. "It's really true, then?"

"Yes, it's true."

"Well, that's the nature of my complaint," I threw at him.

"Oh?" he said. "You have a complaint?"

"Yes. If they eat them, then those dogs are ship's stores. Am I right?"

"Yes, I guess you could say that," he acknowledged. "I guess you could say those dogs are ship's stores. Although I understand they take most of them back to the islands and that they are consumed there."

"Okay," I continued, "but wherever they eat them, the dogs are cargo. Right?"

"Yes. Yes, you might say the dogs are cargo."

"Okay. The dogs are cargo. But we longshoremen aren't loading those dogs. The Filipino crewmen are. Now, why are you, our business agent, letting the crewmen get away with doing our work? That's a violation of the union contract." I had managed to keep a straight face through all this.

The business agent stared at me for a moment, expressionless, and then, without taking his eyes from me, reached out and stopped the crew member, who had just arrived at the foot of the gangplank. The two poodles were trying to go in all directions. One, between escape attempts, would dart back and sink his teeth in the crewman's pants leg, savagely shaking his head from side to side in an effort to jerk something loose. The other dog appeared to be trying to jump into the Bay. Taking the leashes from the startled crewman, the business agent placed them firmly in my hands.

"Okay, son," he said. "You're a longshoreman. You take these dogs up the gangplank."

Ten, fifteen years ago, this was my work. Quite often it was very hard work. But you set your own pace, and since in those days all longshoremen worked together in gangs, you had someone to talk with while you heaved the cargo around. In between loads while waiting for the hook you might even have a can of beer, especially if they were loading it somewhere on the ship. In those days the hold men and gang dock men numbered fourteen and there were five to eight gangs to a ship. If you counted gang bosses, forklift drivers, winch drivers, car men, and clerks, there would be close to 150 men working a pier.

An average gang would turn out 150 to 200 tons each shift. The stevedore companies always liked the higher figure, but they were careful not to push you too hard, because if they did they might end up with the lower. Gang bosses rarely got on the men for more production, unless they were bucking for promotion to walking boss, the next step in the order. Then, if a gang boss spent a lot of time down in the hold of the ship, it was usually because that was where the action was and he preferred being down there to standing around up on deck. If a walking boss came down the ladder and got on your back once too often, you could always tell him to go to hell, collect your gloves, your jacket, and your hook, and go back to the hiring hall and get another job.

From my first day on the waterfront I looked forward to going to work. Most of the men I worked with did, too, although most of them were reluctant to admit it and would do so only in private. Not even coffee, bananas, or hides were all that bad if you caught a good gang.

Recently I worked a container ship, loading vans in the

Port of Oakland. There are no holds or hatches on a container ship; the cargo goes into "cells" and nobody goes down into them, just forty-foot container vans. The "Portainer" crane picks the container, usually weighing between twenty and thirty tons, off the bed of a truck on the dock, swoops it way up over the side of the ship, and drops it down into a cell. The crane driver lowers the container all the way down the cell to the bottom of the ship, releases the van by pushing a button, and comes back out. He puts six vans, one on top of the other, in each cell before he reaches deck level. There are ten cells, reaching from rail to rail, across the vessel. The ship I was working on had fourteen rows of cells. After all the cells are full across the breadth of the ship, the crane driver lowers a huge, one-piece steel cell cover in place and then starts loading containers four or five high on deck. Because of the contours of the ship, however, not all cells can hold the same number of vans. This ship could carry a few over six hundred forty-foot containers. It was a medium-sized container ship.

When a crane driver drops his first container into a cell, his immediate work is only half done. He moves his crane over to the adjoining cell and picks up a van of incoming cargo. He deposits that container on the empty trailer of the truck from which he picked up the previous container. Loading and discharging take place at the same time. What you have on the dock is a constantly moving line of trucks towing trailers carrying vans. The crane takes a van in and brings a van out. In and out . . . in and out. Beautiful, if that sort of thing turns you on.

The only lashing (tying-down of vans) on a container ship is done above deck. The vans below deck are held solidly enough in their cells so that no damage is done to them during the voyage. Above deck, however, the vans, exposed to the weather and stacked one on top of the other five high, have to be securely lashed down. This is done with three-quarter-inch wire cable or rods and large, heavy turnbuckles. The lashers, two men on top of the vans and anywhere from four to eight on deck below, attach the wires to all four corners of the top vans. Then they hook the turnbuckle into the deck and start tightening down. There can be no slack. When you are through with the turnbuckle and you whack the wire, it has to sing.

Sometimes you get breaks during lashing, but usually you do not. When the crane is loading vans below, the lashers have to get the wire rods and turnbuckles ready for use on the deck. When the first deckload of vans is in place across the width of the ship, you begin lashing while the crane moves on to the next row. Lashing begins when two top men lower a light manila line with a small steel hook attached to the end. If you are working below, you hook on a cable and stand back out of the way while the top men pull it up. After the wire is in place above, you rig a turnbuckle into a tie-down welded to the deck. Then you slip the knob at the end of the cable into the turnbuckle and begin cranking away.

It is hard work, since the wire and turnbuckles are heavy and in between the rows of containers it is cramped, and also slippery from the grease that unavoidably falls to the deck from the equipment above. Moving about while you work means picking your way over rigid turnbuckles or squeezing through the thin triangles that the wire makes with the ends of the vans. Hard hats are mandatory. If a lashing falls, pray that it hits your hat and that you do not get caught on the side of the head with the knob at the end of the cable. When the knob comes down, it snaps, like the end of a whip.

This pretty much describes the work of lashing vans on the deck of a container ship. When you finish one row of vans, there is usually another row waiting for you. It takes a fast crew of lashers to stay ahead of a crane. There are still freighters around, and a lot of combination ships that load containers on deck and general, break-bulk cargo below, but these ships are gradually being eliminated. Container ships are also getting larger. Just as the first container ships eliminated a half-dozen freighters because of the speed of loading and discharging cargo and the consequent saving in turnaround time, so does a big container ship eliminate two smaller ones. Ships carrying eleven hundred vans are now coming into port, and on the drawing boards are plans for vessels that will carry eighteen hundred. If the natural progression toward bigness continues, the combined maritime fleets of the world will eventually total about six ships. One for each ocean.

Other than those eight or ten lashers and the truck drivers and the crane operator, there are only two other longshoremen working the ship. These are the dock men. They position themselves on either side of the traffic lanes beneath the crane. When the truck pulls between them they release clamps on the bed of the rig, freeing the van so that the crane can lift it away. When the crane comes back out and sets down the van being discharged, they clamp it back down so the driver does not lose his load when he drives off. Lashing down vans aboard ship is considered a bad job by most longshoremen, but it is much preferred to working on the dock. Alternating back and forth between the row of moving trucks, the dock men have their hands full as they move down either side of the container, releasing latches. Occasionally when they meet at the tailgate of the truck they might say hello, but as soon as the last latch is released they have to move on to the next truck and begin all over again while the crane snatches the first container up and wings it away.

Nobody likes to have twenty tons sailing over his head, so at the beginning of a shift you usually get the hell out of the way between loads, retreating to one end or the other of the crane. But no one can move that fast that often all night long, so sooner or later you just give up, remaining where you are and taking your chances. Hard hats are required on the dock, too. For protection in case a van falls on you, I suppose.

Some companies use straddle trucks instead of tractor trailers to pick up the vans and bring them under the hook. Straddle trucks do just that: the operator drives over and straddles the van. He then lowers a bridle carriage and locks into the four corners, picks the van up, and carries it away. Although straddle trucks move slower, they are more dangerous, because the driver, perched on top of his rig, high above the van, cannot always see what is below him. For this reason straddle trucks are equipped with a warning device, a little horn that goes beep, beep, beep, to let you know a truck is approaching. The only trouble with this is that the crane has a similar warning device, and if the crane driver moves to make a small lateral correction, he goes beep, beep, beep, too. Then you have beep-beeps coming, beep-beeps going, and beep-beeps over your head. The trick is not to let yourself get hypnotized by all the beeps, but to tune in so that you do not get run over or crushed and end up as the meat in a container sandwich. Of course, the equipment operators are always revving their motors, making it impossible to hear anything anyway.

Occasionally through the work shift one does get a respite. Every now and then, for some inexplicable reason, a truck with a container will pull out and no other one will pull in to take its place. The aluminum wall of the van gliding past your nose is suddenly no longer there, and you and your partner, separated by the width of a truck bed, find yourselves alone in the quiet, standing there staring at each other. When this happens it is always debatable whether or not to walk over and speak. If another rig comes in while you are together, one of you will have to hurry all the way around to the other side of the van to get back to his work. You walk over anyway. He asks you what time it is.

"Nine-thirty," you tell him.

"Good. Here comes the coffee wagon."

If you are working nights you get a fifteen-minute break midway through the evening, an hour for your meal period, usually at eleven o'clock, and fifteen minutes again toward morning. The coffee truck is usually there early in the evening. Sometimes it comes at eleven or midnight. But you never see it again after that. And for good reason: why should anyone get up at two o'clock in the morning to sell ten or fifteen men a cup of coffee, which does not even pay for gas money?

After you get your coffee you can stand around and talk to each other or go inside a small coffee room and try to find a seat on a crowded bench. Once inside the shack, a lot of the men immediately fall into that half-trance, half-sleep state that many workingmen seem to have acquired the ability to slip into whenever they have a minute or two to escape from the job. A few men talk, and there is always the inevitable foursome that will try to play a hand or two of cards.

During the meal break it is the shack again for the men who pack their own lunch, or a cold sandwich if the coffee wagon is there. Most men jump into their cars and take off for a restaurant. If you work days, the nearest place to eat is *three miles away*. Ten years ago in both Frisco and Oakland there was a workingmen's restaurant at the head of just about every pier. Although the Port of Oakland is one of the larger container ports of the world, the incredible fact is that because of the automated nature of the work, there are not enough men employed in the several container operations there to support one eating establishment.

On the West Coast, longshoremen have an eight-hour guarantee. This means that when we turn to, if the ship gets its cargo loaded in five or six hours and then sails, we get paid for a full shift, even if we go home early. When we turned to on my recent container-ship job, the first thing we heard was that we were going to get done early. The walking boss came up to our little group standing by the shack and told us this in the manner of someone relating very good news. After he left, two of the longshoremen turned to me.

"What do you think?" they asked.

"Bullshit," I said.

"They say we have only a hundred and sixty-eight vans to move to complete the ship," one of them insisted. "They say we can be out of here by two o'clock."

"Bullshit."

"Yeah," the other man agreed. "They're just trying to jack us up . . . get us to work faster."

One thing that has not changed over the years on the

San Francisco waterfront is that if you do not want to work you do not have to work. I can still tell a walking boss to shove it and nothing much will happen to me. I can call the night dispatcher for a replacement, and that is the end of it. Except that I will lose a night's pay.

On the way back to the ship from the meal break, all four of us in the car expressed a desire to call it quits. But none of us did. The effect of automation is that there are fewer jobs, which in turn means that there is more competition for the jobs that remain. Working nights, we are all getting an average of about three shifts a week. Neither I nor any of the other men lashing containers that night could afford to lose the work. Nevertheless, when we returned from the meal break, the man working with me on the dock and I chose to slow down the operation. Very soon the crane was waiting on us, the carriage hanging over our heads as we slowly walked down the side of the container, flipping latches. Soon after that the walking boss was beside me, standing first on one foot and then the other.

"Hey. For Christ's sake, hurry up!" he shouted in my ear.

"What did you say?" I demanded, turning on him. He knew the rules as well as I do, and they do not include ordering a speedup. That night, like every other night, had started off fast. Then it had accelerated to a pace approaching hysteria. The trucks were tearing ass up and down the pier, the crane was going beep, beep, beep, and twenty tons of cargo was zooming off over our heads. "What did you say?" I demanded again.

He immediately became defensive. "Jesus Christ," he almost pleaded. *"Let's hurry up. Let's hurry up so we can get the hell out of here."*

CHAPTER THIRTEEN

Hey, Quit Your Bitchin'! You're Learning a Trade!

In the 1840s when the sun-baked bird manure on the islands off the west coast of South America was discovered to be valuable, the heavy nitrate content being in demand for both fertilizers and explosives, it attracted shipping from all over the world. The bird droppings—guano—had built up over thousands of years until in some places the deposits were over two hundred feet thick. There were no docks or piers on these islands, and the stuff had to be loaded into small boats and rowed out to the square-rigged merchantmen waiting at anchor.

Initially the ship's crews worked the guano, digging it out of the hillsides on the islands and also stowing it aboard ship. The smell was awful. Worse, pulverized by the pick-and-shovel work the stuff rose in acrid clouds about the men digging and lodged in their eyes and throats, blinding and choking them.

After a few years, Chinese coolies were imported to replace the seamen working ashore. In 1862 the second mate of a Boston ship, the *Astria,* reported that the Chinese, working naked in the hot sun, were in such

poor condition that he believed they would rather die than
live, but that their guards watched them so closely they
could not do away with themselves. "When one does die,"
the mate reported, "they throw a little guano over him,
which the dogs and vultures tear away and then pull him
to pieces. All over the graveyard may be seen heads and
legs of the poor wretches." There were approximately one
hundred ships waiting at anchor when this letter was written. Sometime after that the Peruvian government, which
received income off the islands, supplied convicts to do the
work. Guano continued to be exported this way until
1923.

These are, I think, the worst working conditions I have
ever heard of. (Jules Verne had his fictional Captain Nemo
recruit his crew from among these convicts after effecting
their escape; their rescue from such hell supposedly
ensured their undying devotion and loyalty. I can believe
it.) However, working conditions vary, and whether they
are viewed as good or not is determined to a great extent
by where and when they are taking place. To someone
working a ten-hour day—very common a generation or
two ago—an eight-hour day might look pretty good, and
nine to five (with an hour for lunch) a pure vacation. Still,
a person today going home nauseated and with a headache
and a stiff neck after only seven hours at a computer termi-
nal does not want to be told how great he or she has it.
Such a person can think of better jobs.

Almost all of us have at one time or another had a job
we hated. Hated but kept working at because we could not
quit, usually because we needed the money. Among those
who could not quit we must also count the coolies and the
convicts. Convict labor over the centuries has for some
reason been more badly used than slave labor, perhaps

because of society's desire for revenge for the felon's perceived antisocial conduct.

Also, slaves, as property, were worth something—they could be sold for money. A slave, although by definition not free, might cling to one hope denied a convict—getting a better master, and perhaps a better job. On the other hand, the slave had no expectation of serving out a sentence or getting a parole. Historically both slave and convict were kept for one end, their labor, and by that assignment society very early revealed clearly how it felt—and perhaps still feels—about work. Nothing was noble there. Furthermore, if the crime excited dread, there was a sentence to match it: twenty years . . . *hard* labor.

Work as punishment still holds currency in much of the world except for America and few other nations where the role of prisons is thought to be one of rehabilitation. In 1993 in California the state spent over twenty thousand dollars per year to incarcerate a man and purge him of his criminal tendencies. In most other places, crime merits punishment, and if possible the prison is expected to pay for itself. The Soviet Union built one of its largest prison compounds, Vorkuta, over enormous coal deposits. There the prisoners lived on top of their work, literally, and worked to live. No coal, no food. Here in America—most parts of America, anyway—work in prison is either physical therapy or a means of keeping the inmates occupied, and prison officialdom is careful not to engage in any kind of manufacturing that would compete with private enterprise on the outside.

Here in America, criminals also are treated much the same for their various crimes in that they all end up in the same jail. That is, whatever their crime, they do their time together. Traditionally, however, political criminals were recognized as requiring special treatment, and in England they were, from the French Revolution on, transported. That is, they were sent abroad, to Australia mostly, but to other places too. Shipping them out of the country was official policy; if they were thrown into jail they might organize the other prisoners, and what mischief might they then create? In England by the 1830s the enclosure acts and the power loom had thrown so many people out of work and created so many paupers that no amount of jails could contain them. The antitechnological movement of Luddism appeared and, to the authorities, threatened revolution. It then became a matter of hysterical urgency to rid Britain of potential recruits to that popular movement of the dispossessed. The crime of vagrancy was dusted off, but the first beginnings of protest prohibited sending men and women halfway around the world for merely *that*. It was a problem easily solved. All the authorities had to do was wait a bit until the hungry vagrant stole a loaf of bread and became a thief. Felons were transported.

France behaved differently. Slightly. The French navy still used galleys with oars, and the need for rowers meant that a lot of French criminals ended up there (remember Victor Hugo's *Les Misérables* and Jean Valjean?). But France transported men, too. Devil's Island off the northeast coast of South America was a functioning prison colony until World War II.

Work as punishment implies a curious equation. Punishment is society's response to a criminal act, and the sentence of "hard labor" was deemed the most severe punishment, short of death, that society could administer. Using this reasoning the vast multitudes of everyday workers all over the earth who were engaged in hard labor all the days of their lives might have asked what crime they had committed. None asked, of course, but the presumption was clear: work is base and degrading and those who do it are equated with slaves and criminals and rightfully assigned to the lowest level of society. It was well into this century before the working classes of the world could shake themselves loose from this evaluation and cease subscribing to their own victimization.

After transportation to the colonies was deemed barbarous and done away with, the English jails were, of course, full. With so many prisoners on hand for the limited amount of productive work available, activities were invented as a substitute. Most of them resembled work only insofar as they were designed to be exhausting and produce sweat. Some, to a modern thinker, in addition to being cruel and inhuman, were clearly warped and crazy and contained a strong element of sadism.

One exercise that continued into the twentieth century made use of a cannonball. Twelve convicts were placed in a circle by guards, and a twenty-pound cannonball was introduced to the ring of men. To the beat of a drum the first man picked the cannonball up from the ground, walked over to the man next to him, and placed it at his feet, and so on around the circle. The drumbeat was increased, and then the guards introduced a second cannonball. And then a third, until there were twelve, one for each man. Keeping in time to the ever increasing drumbeat, the men picked up the cannonballs at their feet, raced to place them at the stations of the men next to them, and then hurried back to grab another one. This was kept up until the men dropped. Frankly, I would rather be transported.

Bad working conditions in my experience do not alone

always impede management's goals, which are high production and low labor costs, and in some instances men
will work enthusiastically in disregard of them. For years
I worked a series of jobs that started every spring in the
lower Rio Grande Valley of southern Texas. I would drive
down there from my base in California and for three or
four weeks my fellow fruit tramps and I would work in a
melon shed packing cantaloupes from eight in the morning until approximately nine or ten at night. Since we were
on piece rate—the more crates we packed the more money
we made—we worked all-out at top speed all day long.
Southern Texas is subtropical, and although full summer
was not yet upon us the temperature and humidity were
already so high that before the day had begun we stood at
our packing benches working sopping wet in our own
sweat.

When the deal in Texas was over there was a job waiting
for us in Yuma, Arizona. Arriving in Yuma after driving
all day and all night (it is fifteen hundred miles), we would
immediately go to work. The Yuma jobs usually started
earlier in the morning, frequently at seven, and went later
into the night. After the Yuma crop was in the crates our
next stop was the San Joaquin Valley of California, where
we started at the lower end near Bakersfield in July and
packed our way north, ending up only a hundred miles or
so from San Francisco in late summer.

The late-summer jobs were, finally, a vacation; we usually worked only about eight hours a day, and quite often
less. Earlier, in July, however, in a little town farther
south, I once worked from seven in the morning until well
after midnight for twenty-two days in a row. The temperature reached 110 degrees most days, the mosquitoes, flies,
and other bugs hovered around us in clouds, and the only

places serving food in that little town had long lines behind every stool waiting for the seat to open up.

Without going any further into the working conditions of cantaloupe packers a decade or two ago in western America, let me simply state that, vile as they were, no one was compelling me or the other fruit tramps to work under these conditions. We could have found other jobs. Furthermore, if I fell out, through fatigue or whatever, there were two other potential melon packers eager to fill my place. In short, my point is that although our working conditions did not equal the direness of the guano shovelers, they approached it, and we voluntarily accepted those working conditions for ourselves. One reason, of course, was money. Money and the wild and free life we led, which, frankly, most men and a lot of women enjoy. When they are young, anyway.

We were paid approximately three times as much as the average skilled American worker was making at that time. Essentially what we did was cram a year's work into four months, and we were paid accordingly.

If it seems to the reader—the cantaloupe-eating reader, that is—that melons every summer are unreasonably expensive, and that now you know why—there is some maniac out there extorting more than a thousand or more dollars a week out of the consuming public for packing them—you will have to look elsewhere for the villain. Labor costs for the entire shed, including sorters, loaders, lidders, dumpers, *and the packers,* never ran more than about a cent and a half a melon when I was working them. Costs are higher today, but not much. Think back to what you paid for a cantaloupe when you last bought one. More to the point, reflect on the fact that there was a group of men out there in America who were willing to accept an incentive to range over three of the largest western states every summer and work under absolutely deplorable conditions to harvest the crop and put the melon on your breakfast plate.

The cantaloupe packers (now almost gone) and the guano shovelers are extreme cases, but it is significant that only one group did their job unwillingly. At first the ships' crews were compelled to work the guano islands, but very soon no one would ship out on a vessel headed that way, so coolies were imported. Then the word got back to China and that source dried up. Finally, it came to convicts, and we do not know how many poor devils died on those manure piles after having been snatched up off the street and convicted on whatever trumped-up charges to provide a continuous supply of labor.

When I was packing melons we made so much money that there were always attempts on the part of the commercial growers and packers—our employers—to replace us with cheaper labor. They just never seemed to get it through their heads that it took a lot of money to get a man to work that hard to save their crop. Out in the West, in Arizona and California, this move on the part of our employers always resulted in a strike, which we usually won. You will understand why we won if you envision a packing shed owner and grower with twelve hundred acres of melons about to get ripe all at once and turn into mush within a few days and a scab crew whose fastest packer is able to get only twenty crates an hour, while the fruit tramp who can pack a hundred crates an hour is about to leave town.

In Texas it was a different story. Going to Texas was always chancy, because of the weather. You might drive all that distance and then a cloudburst would rain you out and destroy the whole crop, leaving you not only high and dry but also maybe flat broke. For this reason we demanded more money for packing cantaloupes in Texas, giving the shipper an even greater reason for trying to replace us with cheaper (and unmotivated) local labor and braceros from across the border. Fruit tramps always arrived in Texas a little tentatively, keeping one eye on the sky for rain clouds and, until the harvest was well underway, the other eye on the packing shed to make sure they had the job promised them when they left California. This finally resulted in a compromise in Texas. In California, everyone who worked on the shed made good money, but in Texas the employers insisted on paying the prevailing hourly rate in that area to the sorters and other less skilled workers on the packing shed. And they succeeded in making it stick. The result was that, other than the packers, no one worked very hard in Texas and the employers had to hire more workers to get the job done.

Considerably more. I once worked on a job in Laredo that, had it been in California, would have meant a total shed complement of thirty to thirty-five employees. One day when the lidding machine broke down, stopping everything, we idle packers began counting the crew. It was hard to do because there were so many of them, but we came up with a total of 152. When the shed boss came by, a California man who had lined me up for the job, I stopped him.

"Cliff?" I asked. "How much are your packing costs?"

"Forty-four cents a crate," Cliff replied, pulling culls out of the melon bin beside me—the sorters were not doing their job very well, in spite of their numbers.

"Forty-four cents?" I could not believe it. "Cliff, I heard

you got your packing done last year in California for
thirty-six cents."

"You heard right," Cliff confirmed. "I keep telling that
to the big shots in the office, but they won't let me bring in
any more western help." Or pay their local people enough
money to motivate them, presumably.

In the light of the cantaloupe packers, the question naturally arises: could the mining and processing of guano
under one system or another of hired worker production
be done enthusiastically? My answer would be yes, of
course. But the incentive would have to be something
considerably more than mere money. Those doing the
work would have to be free, and they would have to have
control over their work.

I have worked in a few places, and heard of several others, where workers controlled the job. They ran the operation, determined production and the pace of work, and
assigned duties among themselves. One example that
immediately comes to mind is in the printing trades. They
are losing their control now, but for over two generations
the typographers would not permit managerial personnel
on the shop floor without permission of the shop steward.
Mining is another example; once you go beneath the surface of the earth, those working there usually pretty much
control things.

Even if they do it very well, at a price competitive with
that of other labor, worker control of the production process is always vehemently and ruthlessly resisted by management. It is in the nature of employers in America (and
probably throughout the world) to do this. Even if production has been such that the unit costs of the product
guaranteed a profit, employers have always bitterly fought

worker control, however slight, of any aspect of their business, even to the point of closing down the plant, moving away, and starting up again in another location. You may, as the slogan at the top of the shop bulletin board states, be a member of just one big happy family and be encouraged to drop suggestions for improvements into the box provided. You may be lured by stock offers (nonvoting stock, of course) to own a share of the business. But even if you have worked in the place for thirty years and all of your life, past and future, is wrapped up in the business, any demand you may make for some decision in running the company will be fought to the death, either yours or the company's.

In addition to running the company free of worker participation, management will, if given the power, mandate the movements and routine of each individual task. Using time-and-motion studies, companies continue, with varying success, to instruct workers in how to perform their jobs, even down to the point of telling them when to get their left hand to cooperate with their right, as if there were not a head in between. Unquestionably, time-and-motion studies can go a long way toward smoothing out an operation by eliminating superfluous movement. The fact is, the worker already knows most of these movements—remember the melon packers? He also knows a few moves that management is not even aware of. But he is not motivated to use them. The reason is the adversary position in which the company has placed him.

The company, finely tuned to production enforced *its* way, is simply trying to get all the work it possibly can out of its workers—add another cannonball—and the workers have no choice but to resist or become victims. From my own experience on the job I can assure the skeptic that almost as much thought and effort go into limiting work as in doing it. This has the effect eventually of destroying the work ethic and turning good workers into bad. Most workers would rather do good work and do it efficiently rather than otherwise. But if this only results in more work for the one doing it, he has become a self-made fool. And a tired one. This is why the vast majority of industrial workers have mixed feelings toward their work.

I am not an advocate of piecework. Melons are unique, and what works for cantaloupe packers will work against the men and women on the assembly line. The cantaloupe packer, by will and application, can do three times as much work as the acceptable norm. If a production worker in autos or steel increased his output today, the increase would be incorporated into his workload tomorrow, at no increase in money or time off. Most companies profess to offer incentives—bonuses, pats on the back, your picture in the company newsletter—for more and better work, but these rewards are regarded as swindles and a scam by the vast majority of their employees and not worth nearly the effort necessary to gain them. And of course those few employees who do respond to this sort of bait are universally despised by the men and women whom they work among.

Confining the worker to merely working—and not *participating*—penalizes everyone, finally. When a company gets into trouble, real trouble, as many companies have in America over the last decade because of superior foreign imports and shabby workmanship at home, it cannot call on its own workers for help, for an honest joint effort to recover its own, its workers', and its nation's economic health. Its workers do not trust it, and their past experiences tell them they are right not to.

Few companies have the slightest knowledge of what kind of production would be possible from their existing machinery and equipment if their workers were truly motivated to produce. Companies, instead of seeking a genuine incentive, have to resort to threats when they get into trouble. We will move away, they tell their people, if you do not accept a wage cut. It is a real threat. And if the wage cut is successfully imposed, the downward spiral begins. More work for less money is a losing bargain for the workers, and the product becomes shabbier and shabbier until the competition takes over and the company goes broke. It was no accident that as Japanese cars got better the Japanese worker's wages went up, while as the American's real wages went down so did the quality of our automobiles. Maybe the Japanese's turn will come, since unquestionably Japan's workers are having a creeping scam practiced on them, too. But the lesson to be learned from the cantaloupe packers for corporations of whatever nationality is to seek an incentive their employees will accept. It is cheaper in the long run.

It can be argued that this may be impossible. The makeup of society, all industrial society wherever in the world it exists, may make it impossible. Karl Marx was unquestionably right when he stated that all things of value and use in the world are the result of labor. Further, in his theory of surplus value he made the undeniable point that under capitalism the worker who created these things of value was paid less for his work than the product of his labor was sold for in the marketplace. Marx also understood that the production of the necessities of life under communism would inevitably place on top of the workers a large superstructure of people, both managerial and bureaucratic, whom the worker would have to support through his labor in addition to maintaining his family and himself.

What Marx failed to understand was that, whether the economy was communist or capitalist, to the worker those people above him would be pretty much the same. Furthermore, the politics of work continued unchanged under communism, with the managers and the bureaucrats urging the workers to increase production for a sum beyond which, they persuaded themselves, the whole applecart would be upset.

Marx, it appears, lacked insight into the reality of day-to-day work, perhaps because he never really held down a job. He originally divided work into two categories: that which is drudgery and that which is fulfilling *(travail attractif)*. Drudgery, he contended early on, would no longer be drudgery under communism because the worker would no longer be alienated. However, the unalienated worker does not automatically become fulfilled, Marx later decided, because material production remains a necessity and freedom exists only beyond it in leisure time.

This reasoning begs some questions. Will work, the work needed to be done in the world to keep it functioning, never be free and fulfilling *(travail attractif)*? If so, how will it be decided who will do this work? Finally, is work's reward only to be found in credited leisure time? (Hell, an American auto worker might reply, even under General Motors we all get vacations.) Marx, and all the Marxist scholars after him, merely danced around this question and continued on, proclaiming themselves humanists through their just schemes for the fair distribution of the world's goods, while leaving unaddressed the worker's existence *vis-à-vis* his job producing these goods.

I have very little knowledge of what it is, or was, like

to work in the communist bloc. That is, I do not know what it was *really* like to hold down a job in the Soviet Union, Poland, Hungary, Czechoslovakia, Bulgaria, or Rumania. In the past we have heard a lot from disgruntled artists, writers, nuclear physicists, Jews attempting to flee to Israel, unhappy Balts and Armenians, etc., but very little comes to us from common, everyday blue-collar industrial workers. With the advent of Solidarity, Poland became to some extent an exception to this. But in spite of my great and sincere admiration for Lech Walesa and his coworkers, I still do not know how they feel about compulsory overtime. Maybe I never will, but I do know that industrial work is much the same throughout the industrial world.

It is undeniable that a worker cannot supervise the distribution of the product of his labor except in the most primitive of societies. The modern industrialized world requires a superstructure of people to distribute the products of its factories and farms. What remains unclear to the worker, however, is why the managerial and bureaucratic class created by this process must invariably end up at odds with the production worker. Further, the distribution of power between these two entities, never even, becomes eventually so one-sided that the only way the workers can achieve parity is to engage in a work stoppage, a strike. And more than likely lose it, too, at least in present-day America.

In the United States over the last fifty years, elaborate machinery has been constructed to maintain what is erroneously called "labor peace." Cooling-off periods, compulsory arbitration, anti–secondary boycott legislation, and a number of other routines and measures swing into action before a worker can say no to his existing wages and conditions and stop working. As this machinery has been enacted and judicially put into play the result has been to prolong the existing work situation while prohibiting the workers from collectively exercising their strength to change it. Since this machinery, to the worker, obviously coincides with the interests of the managers over him, he must conclude that there is a direct linkage between the two.

Many of these strike-delaying tactics are presented to the workers as "friendly legislation" in that the workers are presumed to want to avoid striking and a delay will prevent a rash act they may later regret. National interest is also invoked, meaning the country itself cannot afford to have a big segment of its coal mines or railroads shut down. Without arguing that the workers' interest may also be the nation's interest, I would say that it is generally true that workers would rather work than strike. I have, however, more than once seen workers so fed up with their situation that in defiance of the law, their bosses, and even their own trade union leadership, they have hit the bricks and said *no* just by raising hell, somewhat like English workers on a rampage at a soccer game.

Although it is deprecated in all official quarters, job action is extremely widespread in America and frequently gets results, probably because it scares the hell out of both management and trade union power structures. But it also lends force to the argument that more repressive measures should be used against the workers, whether police actions with clubs and tear gas or the kid-glove routines of injunctions, fines, and restraining orders. It also reinforces the deeply held conviction among the establishment that what it is doing is right.

We workers are still, to the vast majority of people

holding power in the world, Louis XVII's "great beast": violent, incapable of self-rule, and best governed by others not of our class, either by deceit or by force. We must be told what to do because we are incapable of even recognizing our own self-interest, and the only government we might be capable of would result in chaos and anarchy. Although there is no record in history of a government run by the workers from which to draw this conclusion, this opinion is, whether voiced or not, universally held by government, corporate, and, yes, trade union leaders and functionaries in America today.

CHAPTER FOURTEEN

Where We Are Now

Emperor Vespasian, engaged in rebuilding Rome after the destructive reigns of Nero, Otho, and Vitellius, was presented by an inventor with plans for a lifting device that would greatly reduce the need for human labor in the reconstruction. Vespasian rejected the machine because it would throw too many men out of work. "I must feed my poor," he said.

One could say that Vespasian here shows a commendable regard for his subjects. He certainly does when compared to the powerful of Victorian England, who totally rejected responsibility for taking care of the poor that they had so systematically created through the enclosure laws and industrialization. Where Victorians come out as complete and utter villains, Vespasian more closely resembles a Roman Franklin Delano Roosevelt creating a WPA for the construction of parks and post offices. Although almost nineteen centuries separate Vespasian and FDR, they had in common that they regarded their tenure as a stewardship, each exercising his power toward a common good as he saw it.

Rome was never democratic at any time and did not profess to be so. But Roosevelt saw things differently and took steps to give American workers some ongoing power over their lives at work, beginning with the Wagner Act and continuing on through other New Deal legislation. American workers were for the first time endowed with the right to organize, to present demands, and to withhold their labor—to strike—if they chose to do so. Their employers, by law, were forced to recognize these as workers' basic legal rights. However, bargaining agents—trade unions—were assigned to represent the workers in their relationships with their employers and workers were encouraged to join them.

The bargaining agent became the supreme instrument through which the workers' hours, wages, and working conditions were determined. Conversely, the work process, with minor exceptions, remained within the purview of the employer. That is, how the actual work was done remained under the total control and direction of the employer. Even a journeyman could be denied input into how to do his job if the boss so chose.

In the following decades and up to the present, the relationship between the trade union and the employer has been expanded and codified into law to the point that American workers cannot function outside of the system. One result has been that in recent years workers have frequently found themselves opposed by both their employer and their union. If the workers attempt to move independently of their trade union they can find themselves opposed by all the forces of the government and are subject to fines and imprisonment if they persist. Furthermore, in conflicts between the rank and file and the union the law tends to support the union power structure and to maintain the status quo.

This can occasionally reach the point of absurdity. Not too long ago, long-haul rank-and-file Teamsters turned down a proposed contract negotiated by their international union by a 65 percent no vote, and the contract was still ratified over their heads by their union president. This was accepted by the government and the courts without a murmur. And this Teamster instance is far from unique. So much for worker democracy.

What FDR and his New Deal colleagues really did, of course, instead of giving workers a bill of rights, was to place them under an expanded stewardship consisting of, in addition to the boss, the trade union leadership and its bureaucracy.

Stewardship is the bottom line here, and in the politics of work what this means is that workers continue to labor under conditions in which their decisions are always subject to overrule by someone else. This situation is not confined to America, of course, but exists throughout the industrialized world.

The communist managers of the Gdansk Shipyard in Poland were not all villains, or at least the testimony of Lech Walesa so indicates. However, even if they had been the most decent, humanistic men imaginable, the mindset they brought to their effort to gain more production from the Polish shipyard workers was essentially the same as that of their capitalist counterparts in the West. That is, they felt themselves to be in an adversary position *vis-à-vis* those workers. Production goals set by five-year plans throughout the communist world consistently went unmet from their beginnings in the middle 1920s. Unquestionably, poor planning and bureaucratic ineptitude had something to do with this, but the glaring fact remains that production goals failed because workers failed to produce. Workers chose not to apply themselves to maximizing their own potential and that of their machines.

That essentially was the failure of the Bolshevik Revolution. That will continue to be the failure of the industrial revolution, because industrial production is similar wherever you choose to examine it throughout the industrialized world under whatever ideology or regime. All production processes at present, worldwide, strive for more production at the expense of the worker. That has become the politics of labor.

We have for the most part passed beyond that point in history where a few members of the human race, possessing either strength or guile or both, forced the rest of mankind to provide them with a living and accumulate them wealth—and then, not content with this bounty, called their victims base and despised them for the work they did on their behalf. Society is more egalitarian now. However, class is still with us, and we are all aware that unknown numbers of people, perhaps an embarrassing number, feel themselves to be above other men and women, starting with those of us who dirty our hands at work. Still others, in America mostly, find a certain status in connecting themselves to work, while carefully avoiding manual labor as a career. I cannot tell you how many times I have sat through an account by some executive of that summer he spent between his sophomore and junior year at college working on a hay baler, or stacking lumber, or you name it.

One would think that early work experience would give an executive greater insight into and understanding of work, the work process, and the people who work. However, closeness to work may not be instructive, and that executive who once stacked lumber may be initiating tyrannies in his factory, office, or department store that are harsh beyond reason.

Recently I witnessed an example of this on a very primal level. The work scene was a wholesale fish plant near Fisherman's Wharf in San Francisco where a group of young women were cracking crab. The work process was a primitive assembly line with the women stationed on both sides of a movable belt. They took the freshly cooked crab from the belt, cracked it, removed the meat, and placed it in cans for sealing and delivery to market.

The women were mostly Pacific Islanders, and I had to marvel at how good they were at what they were doing. Their hands flashed back and forth so fast I could barely follow them as they separated the crabmeat from the shell. All the while they worked they burst forth with bits of conversation punctuated with giggles, cries, shrieks, and laughter. As I watched, one of the owners of the small plant pushed a four-wheel cart loaded with full boxes through two swinging doors. He dumped more crab on the belt and moved it in front of the women.

"Hey!" he said severely in a loud voice. "Less talk. Let's see more work around here and less noise." He waited awhile before he left, and the women, their smiles gone, settled down into a dull, silent, slow routine. What ugly thought process, I wondered, possessed that man to feel that he had the authority to demand that those women stifle their laughter.

I have seen similar things happen many times in workplaces turning out much more sophisticated products. When workers find ways of introducing mirth and play into their drudgery, silent forces invariably move to criticize. Laughter is a sign that waste is present, that not all effort is being devoted to production. People have been taken off the assembly line and sentenced to be alone in isolated places of work because of it.

Every revolutionary, from Christ to the Bolsheviks to the latest one to rise up last week, aspires to recast man. As modern work has evolved, those people who have achieved the direction of it have attempted to redesign men and women (other than themselves, that is) for production purposes. A curious footnote to this is the failure in the western world of those who, for want of a better word, must be called "the bosses" to learn from past experience and see what is in front of their faces: even in a capitalist market economy a worker-run production system makes more sense, since production is enhanced.

Industrial workers are at present alienated from their work. The alienated worker performs dutifully, perhaps, but with little enthusiasm. Without enthusiasm, optimum production is never achieved, and reduced attention to quality results in an increasingly shoddy product. If American products are to compete with foreign products—Japanese products, say—then American workers must be freed to produce enthusiastically.

Worker enthusiasm comes to pass in more than one way. Money is important, and I have seen it generate a lot of enthusiasm. But doubling every worker's wages would merely debase the currency. Devotion was once a factor. Perhaps it can be again, but I do not see anything on the horizon in our world that might approximate the religious zeal that built the cathedrals of the Middle Ages. Secular devotion of the kind one used to see in individual craftsmen, meticulously turning out a quality product with skill and efficiency, is absent in the modern factory. That craftsman working today in that mode would merely have his workload increased until finally, in frustration and bitterness, he would sacrifice quality and take steps to limit his output.

Japanese work habits are today cited as an example of what can be accomplished in a modern factory. As much as American and European industrialists might like to impose them in their own factories, those work habits are probably the one thing in Japan that cannot be exported. The Japanese resemble no people found anywhere in the West. Although we know they have classes, in Japan it is as if class conflict, at least to any significant degree, does not exist, not to mention class warfare. They have had an industrial revolution in which no one feels exploited. In Japan production, efficient production, has become a religion to which everyone subscribes, with all energies directed toward the refined application of intensive work to produce objects to be sold somewhere else.

Japan's avid pursuit of world markets while closing its own takes national socialism one step further to national capitalism. Stumbling back in bewilderment from defeat in a war their national pride and character told them they could not lose, Japan's leaders directed the country on a course to outdo the West in what the West did best. In Japan, production is on a perpetual war footing, but for the Japanese worker, toward what end? The reward of an annual two weeks in Hawaii in return for long hours of breakneck drudgery throughout the rest of the year is poor compensation for the person on the Japanese assembly line.

The significance of Japanese production methods for American workers is that it once more places them in competition with other workers, this time foreign. To the leaders of American industry, more production from American workers for the same or lesser pay is the main solution to foreign competition. Industrial technology is essentially equal worldwide, or capable of being so. If American workers took up this challenge and surpassed every nation in the world in industrial output, every foreign industrial nation, starting with Japan, would be urging its own workers onward to greater heights of production to catch the Americans. To what end, for all workers, other than increased fatigue and drudgery? Workers competing with workers—of whatever nationality—results in worker victimization. Most workers know this. Those who do not know it do not remain ignorant forever—at least in the West. Japan is an unknown to us, not being an heir to western history and traditions. Will its industrial workers continue as they are at present, or will they come up with perhaps an even better answer than their western brothers and sisters have to offer?

The first and immediate response to the suggestion that those who do the work be included as full partners in the production process is that it would never work. Workers, the argument goes, will never do anything they do not have to do. They will take advantage of a position of equality to lie down on the job and collect their wages without earning them. Everything will grind to a halt. Workers are naturally recalcitrant and lazy, and respond with action only when compelled to do so. The present modes of production are the best that can be hoped for. Mankind must go forward into eternity producing the goods and services of the world using the process of reward and punishment, the carrot and the stick, that is currently in force.

This depressing vision of the future of humanity, in which 90 percent of the people have to be driven or bribed by the other 10 percent or things will not function, condemns itself not merely by its institutionalized elitism and its acceptance of the exploitation of the many by the few, but more crushingly by its gloomy outlook for mankind. It contains no hope for the future. We now live in the best of all possible worlds. What you see around you, except for some small adjustments and fine-tuning, like consolidating jobs and jacking up the pace of the assembly line, is what we will always have. Nothing more. This condemns those who produce and those who control the means of production to constant friction and an adversary position forever.

I have no doubt that upon being incorporated into the production process as equals many individual workers would at first take advantage of a self-directed work situation to grab a free ride. Two hundred years of exploitation will make trust less than forthcoming, especially at first. But very quickly, as worker empowerment becomes real, the rest of the crew will shape up anyone who is dogging it. Actually, in self-directed work situations in which I have been involved, many times the other members of the work team have been harder on the goof-off than the boss would have been in a management-controlled situation. Another problem would resolve itself, about which all good workers are now ambivalent: the solidarity on the job that now requires protecting a bad worker against the boss simply because he is a fellow worker. Anyone dragging his feet cannot justify his conduct when those he injures are primarily himself and the others with whom he works.

To maintain that workers are incapable of self-direction

in the jobs they do is quite simply a manifestation of class prejudice enhanced by feelings of superiority—and probably feelings of fear, by those members of the white-collar class whose importance in the world, not to mention income, is dependent upon their role as administrators over some contingent of blue-collar workers. Render a boss superfulous, and what has he got left? It also implies that workers left to themselves are inherently susceptible to indolence and sloth, and probably venality and theft. All this from those strata of society that include not only double-bookkeeping accountants and other white-collar criminals but those captains of industry and commerce who daily pollute our air, rivers, and seas, and steal people's savings and retirement funds—over $200 billion at last count—through savings and loan swindles. I would also add those manipulators of industry who have disrupted and nearly destroyed whole regions of our country by closing factories and relocating them abroad. All of these stalwarts are, at the very least, morally ill equipped to pass judgment on someone else. Character is character wherever one finds it.

The final answer to those who support the labor-management division as it currently exists is that they cannot know if full worker equality would fail in the workplace because it has never been tried, at least not honestly on a large scale. To my knowledge there are no examples in history of a continuing worker direction of a production process within the mainstream of an industrial society. The few examples of large-scale blue-collar takeover of the workplace failed not because of worker indolence, but because of the sheer weight of the counterforces mustered against them by owners, directors, and financiers. There are actual instances of workers bringing guns into the factory in an attempt to maintain possession of the machinery and plant that they had recently won. They were defeated, and rather quickly, but by greater firepower, not by indolence or lack of determination.

There are numerous examples, however, of workers gaining control over some segment or process of work within the larger society in which they live. On examination, these instances reveal a remarkable similarity of pattern and outcome. They invariably start in a work situation that is functioning only barely successfully, or perhaps failing outright. The managers are at wit's end, and I can state from my own experience that what they do in this situation is oversupervise. They are everywhere, frantically rearranging work in an attempt to get more output, contributing more to the general confusion than to increasing production. Finally, the workers enter the picture. They may be asked in by a desperate management. More likely they will get together and confront management with its failure and offer to help, unquestionably, at least in part, to save the enterprise and consequently their own jobs. I have personally been present and taken part in situations like this. I have heard about many more.

What happens next is that the workers make demands and exact a price for their participation. Their first demand always is that management get the hell out of the way and let them get on with the work unimpeded. Their price will come later. It may be more money, but more than likely an existing bargaining agreement will bind them to their present pay scale. Unquestionably it will include more control over what happens to them when the job is done, when their success is apparent. Management usually accedes to these terms, reluctantly perhaps, but since nothing else is succeeding, management gives it a try.

When management accepts the terms, vague though they may be, the increase in production is immediate and dramatic. Nobody knows how to work like a worker, and when workers work in cooperation with each other the results can be astonishing. A recent example of this phenomenon that has come to my attention occurred among a group of men working out of the longshore local in Los Angeles.

Containerization in ocean shipping has now reached the point that the flow of goods in twenty- and forty-foot containers, or "cans" as they are called, continues uninterrupted from their port of origin in the Orient to their final destination somewhere in the vast hinterlands of America. Upon the vessel's docking at one of the West Coast ports, for example, a good portion of the discharged containers are trucked directly to a marshaling yard and loaded aboard flatcars to make up a train for their journey inland. In Los Angeles one of these staging areas, newly set up, was manned by twelve men and women. Their job consisted of loading and lashing down forty-foot vans on railroad flatcars, sometimes two high, using thirty-five-ton forklifts and straddle trucks. Rather a straightforward piece of work, it would seem. However, the operation could not get itself sorted out, and production was failing to achieve the results anticipated by management, which had hoped to make up a hundred-car train daily and do it in eight hours, ten if necessary. After three weeks of concentrated effort, the staging area workers were not getting their train out, even working the two hours overtime. What finally happened was related to me by the president of the Los Angeles longshore local.

Local officers of longshoremen's unions on the West Coast of America can serve in office for only two years, and then they have to go back to work and get dirty again. In Los Angeles after an equal time back working they can run for reelection.

"I had just been reelected," my informant said. "I was trying to get a grasp on things, and I got this phone call from an old work buddy of mine.

" 'Mr. President,' he said, 'you'd better get your ass down here. Things are falling apart.'

"I knew about the operation, but I hadn't checked it out. I knew it was important to us, too, to the local—automation is cutting the hell out of us, as usual, and twelve jobs is twelve jobs. So I went out to the installation.

"You won't believe it," he continued, "but they had fourteen supervisors if you counted in the clerks and walking bosses along with the executives. Fourteen chiefs for twelve indians. I got the guys together with the head honcho, a man named Wilson. I told Wilson he wasn't getting anywhere and he'd better listen to these people doing the work. 'Okay, you guys,' Wilson says, 'what's on your mind?'

"They all started talking at once, and they all said about the same thing: get all these supervisors the hell out of the way and let us do it our way.

" 'What's your way?' Wilson asked.

" 'Don't jam us,' one of the lift drivers said.

" 'Have the clerks spot the vans ahead of time, but don't feed them to us until we call for them,' another said. 'If you haven't got the van yet, we'll leave the space and fill it later.' You know, everybody had ideas.

" 'Okay,' Wilson agreed. 'We can give it a try. But what do you guys want?'

"I knew what they wanted, so I told him right out: 'The men already have an eight-hour guarantee. If they get the job done early, they get to go home early with the full day's pay.'

" 'Yeah, and no bitching about it afterward,' someone said.

" 'I'll tell you what,' Wilson said. 'It's now two-thirty. If you guys get this train out, I'll give you the whole ten hours . . . including the two overtime, no matter what time you finish.'

"The guys got the train out by five-thirty. I came by again the next afternoon about three. They had already got the train out and gone home. Wilson was there. You know what he said to me?"

"What?" I asked.

" 'Thank you.' "

CHAPTER FIFTEEN

Sisyphus's Rock

It was once said by a seventeenth-century English political philosopher that the life of man in primitive societies was nasty, brutish, and short. If instead of looking backward several thousand years to prehistoric humans he had looked ahead a couple of centuries to the industrial worker of nineteenth-century England, he could have made the same observation.

Modern man is less than perfect, and admittedly many examples of him slip below the brutish to the criminal, but we all generally agree on what would constitute an ideal community of men and women in the world and profess with some sincerity to strive toward that end. What was the civilizing factor that started that early primitive human on the road to the goal that we are still plodding toward today?

The immediate and apparent value of primitive work, of course, lay in the gathering of food and the creation of shelter—objects of need that required the cooperation of everyone, large and small. Many animals were better hunters than primitive man, and many more were better adapted to the heat and cold of their environments. But it was only *Homo sapiens* that progressed toward civilization. Any number of creatures crop grass and forage for seeds to eat, but it was only man who planted a field of wheat. And it takes two to raise a roofbeam. Perhaps early man's physical shortcomings forced him to have a more cooperative attitude toward other men simply to survive.

Cooperation in common tasks moved mankind beyond the symbiosis of mere need to a sense of the future and how to prepare for it. Common work was the civilizing factor that led man up from brutishness, and the potential of a world achieved through cooperative work engendered friendship, warmth, and all the qualities we call human. In spite of all our progress, however, the demands of the modern workday still make it impossible to fully experience and express these feelings, the best that are within us. Insofar as this is denied the modern worker on the job, the modern factory is irrational.

Work is always rational, or always tends toward being so. Work processes are always rational, or, where they are not, workers always tend to try to make them so. Left alone, workers and work tend toward perfection, unless corrupted by influences outside the work scene—abuse, manipulation, exploitation, all those practices which have been catalogued so repeatedly over the years that we know them by heart. The perfect work scene does not now and may never exist. But every production process sooner or later is compelled to measure itself against its own ideal. All, of course, are found wanting, some more so than others.

In each of those areas where the production process experiences failures, however small, production suffers and fails to achieve its maximum. Without the complete and enthusiastic participation of every worker, free to achieve his or her own potential, no production process can even approach its ideal. Consequently, in all work situations where the production process takes place at the expense and denial of human values, production suffers. Everywhere in the world today, but most especially in America, workers find themselves holding ambivalent feelings toward the work they do. Because of this they do their work at less than their potential—that is, they work, at least to some extent, irrationally.

This worker ambivalence, which some call worker recalcitrance, had its start back at the beginning of the industrial revolution and the factory system. We no longer work twelve hours a day and die young, but we toil with hardly more enthusiasm than did those early miners and mill hands. Now we have pensions, annual vacations, and good teeth—at least those among us who belong to strong trade unions with dental plans do—and we got all this by adopting an ongoing adversarial position toward those controlling the means of production. We keep it by periodically threatening to shut down or interrupt those same means of production. Despite the sophisticated tools and processes brought to the modern workplace by modern technology, this constant state of warlike tension has remained essentially the same as it was a century and a half ago. Progress has been made in the hardware but not among the human beings. Common sense would seem to indicate that a reexamination of this wasteful, antihuman, antiproduction dynamic is long past due. To go on as we have, still locked into the nineteenth century, means a continuation of waste, unemployment, anger, and alienation—in short, a clinging to irrationality.

Karl Marx's genius was in seeing that unbridled capitalism, that is, the exploitation of one person by another, was fundamentally irrational, that its fundamental exploitive features of rewarding one group for the work of another would continually (historically) lead to social dissonance and civic upheaval. Marx's mistake, and I use the word humbly, was his failure to see that the destruction of capitalism might lead to its replacement by a political system equally exploitive of the workers and with perhaps even fewer rewards, as exemplified by the bureaucratically run communist states of post–World War II eastern Europe and the Soviet Union. Perhaps it may be that it takes a worker to see and anticipate this, and as I pointed out earlier, Marx never held down a job.

Work is undeniably needed as much in the modern world as it ever was in the ancient.* Despite the advent of automation and robotics, more people are employed now than ever before. What then must be done not only to restore and keep the best that is human in the workplace but to enhance production? The answer, of course, is to incorporate workers into the production process. Fully.

This must not, cannot, be done by any violent revolutionary process. Revolution has been subscribed to and attempted by groups of workers and others over the years and has always resulted in the replacement of one repressive state by another. What must be done is to turn over the production processes to the workers themselves because it is in the self-interest of everyone, not just the

---

*I am speaking practically, not psychically. It has been argued, especially by a number of nineteenth-century Germans, that work is essential to man's mental health. I would not deny that, but I am here confining myself to the mundane.

workers but *everyone,* to do so. Work is done best by those who do it daily.

Historically the idea of the need for a hereditary ruling elite has been discarded by everyone, except a few remaining would-be monarchs and their attendant hopefuls. The American and French revolutions began this turn away from hereditary rulers, and creeping democracy is completing the job. The original ten amendments—the Bill of Rights—to the United States Constitution are now up to twenty-six as more people have over the years been brought into fuller partnership in the Republic. Nevertheless, a glance into those areas where America has failed seems to suggest that we will be adding several more amendments before the Constitution has achieved perfection. However, there is more to it than merely giving those sleeping in doorways an address so they can vote.

Any system of beliefs codified in a constitution that embodies a promise of freedom and equality for everyone will, as an ongoing process, be measured against the status quo. If the status quo is found wanting, there will be persistent attempts to bring it and the constitution into harmony, to fulfill its promise, by those citizens whom it has failed, left out. The progress, however slow, toward racial and sexual equality in America has proved this. Similarly, industrialization and its attendant development automation contain, have always contained, an implied promise of more happiness for everyone, workers most of all. Measured against the status quo on the present-day assembly line, this promise has not yet been kept. Measured against the 1960s, perhaps the high-water mark for American workers up to now, we have been slipping backward—temporarily, one hopes. In the area in which I live, only one worker in eight can now afford to purchase his own home. In the mid-1960s a worker could put himself and his family into a new three-bedroom, two-bath house for a down payment of two or three hundred dollars, the equivalent then of his vacation pay or less, with the monthly mortgage payment the rough approximation of one week's wages, which he earned by working no more than forty hours. Clearly, some new ruling ethic or elite, more systematic, more dedicated, cold, and anonymous, has insinuated itself into power and reversed the slow progress of American workers. This has not happened without great harm and cost to our country. Those thrown out of work and on the dole are either apathetic or bitter, and among the working people who are now poorer, absenteeism and wildcat strikes are increasing annually. Of equal importance and finally more destructive of America and, consequently, the workers themselves is that on the job nobody does more than he has to.

There is nothing about History that says things have got to get better. We have too many instances of things getting worse. But there appears to be on the part of humans ongoing attempts—a drive, if you will—to solve our problems as these problems arise. However, the problems surrounding work, how we do it and what it does to us as we do it, its rewards and lack of the same—its agony—remain little better resolved than they were 150 years ago. They remain, in fact, unaddressed. All that has really happened over time is that refinements of tools and techniques have taken place that are designed to get the world's work done more quickly—by someone else, of course.

There is nothing inherently wrong or evil about the invention or perfection of better tools, but automation, like all previous production processes, has been accompanied by a rigid political premise, too. Any and all power and control over this work process is carefully denied those essential to making it function, the workers. In fact, it has now become clear that those who control the means of production are completely aware of what they are doing and prefer to continue producing in the traditional inefficient, irrational, and costly way rather than share this power over the machine with those who tend it, the workers. Until this basic political fact is recognized, addressed, and resolved, work processes will remain crippled, limping on into the future. And on the job there will continue to be waste, inefficiency, and uncooperative, angry, and alienated workers.

America's history, starting when the Pilgrims stepped ashore at Plymouth Rock, has been marked with milestones of progress. Anyone who has taken a high school civics class knows by heart what they are. But along with the popular vote, the Thirteenth, Fourteenth, and Fifteenth Amendments, and the enfranchisement of women, we also have achieved child labor laws, a minimum wage, and the eight-hour day, equal milestones in the nation's progress and measures of its well-being. If any attempt were now made to disenfranchise women or reenslave black Americans, riot and revolution would immediately follow. These rights are as solid as the Lincoln Memorial and Plymouth's original rock. But despite enormous increases in production through automation, most workers in America today are not making a living working eight hours. If the husband / father is not moonlighting, his wife is filling the gap with, at the least, a part-time job. And the minimum wage has become a license to staff fast-food establishments with cheap labor—teenagers whose livings are subsidized by their families, who provide them with homes. No mainstream adults are found working at fast-food counters, and not merely because one cannot make a living there. They simply are not hired as a matter of policy.

Policy is policy to management, and in order for it to continue to be self-serving, it must be extremely rigid. Most of the time it appears to the workers involved that management is working against its own self-interest. But management has its reasons, and they are not always tied to production. Control is a factor. As a footnote to the account of the work in the marshaling yard where train-loads of ocean containers were made up for their trip east, I must report that the superintendent who agreed to the workers' solution, and achieved overwhelmingly success-ful production goals, was very shortly discharged—fired. And the man who replaced him soon met the same fate, as did two others who followed him. Each was assigned rigid production goals, but an even more rigid production pol-icy of control prohibited each from achieving that output.

Researching work by reading history is not very rewarding. In the ancient world and up until fairly recently, class lines were less flexible than at present and most historians regarded physical labor as so far beneath them that they disdained recording it. But also common work has been so much present over the centuries that very likely it was simply taken for granted, dismissed instead of described. For whatever reason, there are very few accounts of workers on record doing the work that workers do. When workers do turn up, their presence invariably is in conjunction with another class. They are the trusty yeoman, the loyal retainer, the gamekeeper, and so forth. Not really workers. Even the French *annales* school of historians, still diligently examining archives of daily village life in fourteenth-century Languedoc, can, while producing volumes on land tenure, tell us very little about working that soil. In the England of that century, Chaucer gives us, in passing, a glimpse of a blacksmith working at night, and then passes on without comment. Later, under Elizabeth I, there is a document, a labor code pertaining to artisans and field laborers. Mostly it confines itself to how much they may charge for work that once again remains undescribed. One noteworthy provision was that since the workday was from dawn to dusk, in winter workingmen were to be paid less, because with less daylight there was a shorter workday.

In researching work, one also has to guard oneself against being overcome by unrelieved depression and gloom. In the eleventh, twelfth, and thirteenth centuries, vast numbers of families roamed the forests of south-central France living principally off the wild chestnuts they could gather. There must have been good times, times of cheer, but the endless accounts of appalling living conditions dominated by hunger and privation and of the individual selfishness imposed by those conditions will, if read without caution, convince the reader that entire centuries passed without a trace of fun or laughter.

If history is barren, literature and myth are not much better in revealing how past workers plied their trade. Piers the Plowman has carried his job description with him down through at least eight centuries, but we do not know the size of the plot of ground he worked, what crop he prepared the land for, or even if he had given the creature he urged down that furrow a name. In literature and art, peasants spend most of their time sitting around a peat or faggot fire being crafty or lascivious instead of out there hoeing those potatoes. Similarly, the labors of Hercules are more heroic than productive.

There is one Greek, however, passed down to us in myth, who is undeniably a worker and whose job is described to us in detail. Sisyphus was condemned by the gods to spend all eternity pushing a heavy stone up the side of a mountain only to have it roll back down again each time he reached the summit. Starting over again each time from the base of that peak, Sisyphus, with his endless, weary, hopeless task, has provided philosophers down through the ages with a symbol of despair for mankind.

A worker placing himself in Sisyphus's shoes will despair, too—but after a little while he will begin to concern himself with the job at hand. I wonder about Sisyphus. Does he, abandoning for a moment the wisdom that previous failed attempts have given him, take heart a bit at discovering on the rock a rough spot that he has never noticed before, A spot where he can get a better grip? And his footing—is it solid enough so that he can crouch down, dig in, and get his shoulder under the stone so that he can *really* shove? Is there a stick of wood around handy that he can grab and throw under the rock to chock it so that he can pause long enough to catch his breath? In short, what does he have to work with? I know what his human condition is, but what are his working conditions? What is the weather like? Is it cold? Is he getting rained on? How old is he? I know he does not have any gloves. When does he eat? Most likely at noon. Here, I know that Sisyphus and I have suddenly bridged the gap between us with a common question. What has the wife packed us for lunch?

9 780393 315578